The Constitution

A Document Steeped in History and a
Compromise Devoid of Promise

Dr. Fred Blanchard

Table of Contents

Preface

Before their adoption of the U. S. Constitution, the States were affiliated with each other through a compact called the Articles of Confederation. Under this agreement, the States remained sovereign and their only differences were the numbers of citizens and the natural wealth each possessed and was originally given to them by the King of England. To loosen themselves from taxation without representation, they agreed to share the cost of pursuing a war against England. The share was based on the only method they had which possessed a degree of accuracy and that was the number of freemen in each State.

Even this measure was not completely accurate because freemen had different meanings in each State. For example, some States, particularly those in the Northeast allowed women the vote and hence they were counted. The consequence of this meant certain States would pay more than their share and others less. The result was that some States paid more, others less and some did not pay at all. Compounding this situation was the fact that the Congress that administered the compact had no means of collecting on its invoices and no means of punishing those who failed to pay, fully or only partially. When the war had been won and the economic ties between the new United States and England severed, it became necessary to adopt an economic system that would pay the debts incurred by the war and one that would restore the economy to order. In particular, it meant paying the debts to foreign lenders so as not to lose the ability to borrow. One must remember the United States had little exchange and its only collateral was the land it won from England.

If the United States were to hang together for its defense it had to have a secure means to finance an administrative apparatus and a navy that would defend each of them from invasion. The efforts of the Marquis de Lafayette are lauded in our schools but the real effort was French naval support all during the war and that of privateers. If a permanent Navy, under U. S. command were to be built and staffed it would take money. An economic system would have to be put in place to insure its initial capital expense and then the need for its ongoing operation and maintenance. As every original colony, now separate sovereignties with a coastline where invaders could land, would benefit from a consolidated navy as opposed to each having their own, economics dictated a combined effort and responsibility. Each State had its own militia and a combined force if necessary was also necessary in the event an individual State was met with a superior force. A centralized military establishment was greatly feared as it could be used by a rogue administration to establish a dictatorship. There was equivalent of need or want but inequality of substance and the only way to measure that inequality was a States wealth and the assumption was made that all freemen were average in wealth and therefore, was the basis on which the shares of a common cost would be shared. It was this false assumption that required the compromises that resulted in the new Constitution of the United States. It began as an agreement by the States to establish a third party, the federal government, for the sole purpose of providing a service (defense) not only of the country as a whole but that of States from each other. In addition, it was to establish monetary and measurement standards for all.

A quorum of 7 States convened on May 25, 1787 and adjourned on September 17, 1787 during which time they debated and fashioned the document that would become the Constitution of the United States. The problems and controversy started almost immediately when Virginia introduced a plan to create a government and not modify the Articles of Confederation as the delegates were sent to do. From that point, it did not deviate when several other delegations submitted alternative plans. The Constitution was the ultimate compromise containing the seeds of its own demise; a government with a charge far beyond what any of them could control and an economic system both of which have doomed all previous governments to ultimate failure.

The following pages illustrate not why they chose the path they did but the machinations necessary to attempt its correction. The problem was it was an impossible task to begin with because the task they set was not the one for which they were charged. In all of history, only the Swiss have come close to the ideal. Most recently they attempted what was necessary from the beginning to create a government that could be limited to its charge and that is the defense of life, liberty and property. I describe this in my latest book, "The Real Economy".

Chapter 1
Taxes

Article 1 Section 8 reads, the Congress has the power "to lay and collect taxes, duties, imposts and excises, to pay the debts and provide for the common defense and general welfare of the United States; but all duties, imposts and excises shall be uniform throughout the United States". The debts of the infant country were those amassed with the issuance of paper (scrip) used to buy the supplies and pay for services provided the government of the Continental Congress and the promissory notes issued to Americans and foreign banks. Like our current debt, none of this paper was backed by gold or silver but "the full faith and credit of the United States". Like the creditors of today, many expected the Continental Congress to redeem this paper, some with interest, once the government could get the States to reimburse the federal government for their rightful share. During the conflict, the States were issued invoices for their share of the cost of the government. Many only paid a part and a few paid none, thereby owing the federal authority the balance of those unpaid invoices. As part of the concessions made in the framing of the Constitution the signatory States agreed to consolidate this debt and allow the federal government to tax all of them equally in order to redeem it and at the same time provide a mechanism for the government to avoid such a debt again by allowing it to tax to pay the ongoing expenses of government.

The strongest argument that can be made for taxes to be only used for the ongoing expenses for the defense and general welfare of the United States is its inclusion in the Constitution as a mechanism to recover the ordinary and necessary costs of government to provide this service to the States. It was a way to enforce payment of each State's share of this cost that was unavailable to the federal authority under the Articles of Confederation. The Continental Congress always had the authority to borrow for this purpose to cover the anticipated payment of the invoices presented to the States, just as the States had this power in order to finance their own governments. The borrowing in both cases was the anticipated amount to be recovered covered annually through state taxes. In common terms these notes are called "tax anticipation bonds", redeemed as the taxes to pay the government's expenditures since they had already been made prior to receipt of the payment of taxes. The State governments were to balance their budgets with this mechanism but any other borrowing was under strict limits as to the amount. The State of Maine, for example, is limited to $2,000,000 unless approved by the people of the state.

Both federal and state governments have engaged in activities not permitted by their constitutions. As a consequence, the expense of government has increased dramatically. The primary ones are pension obligations, welfare payments to individuals and now healthcare. These are all individual obligations and not the responsibility of government. The government has taken on these responsibilities because our economic system, that requires one to work in order to survive, cannot accommodate the expense of the larger number who cannot work. This includes children, the infirm and the elderly who cannot compete with younger workers for the paying jobs available. This economic system evolved when nature's assets once shared equally by all became the property of individuals who then determined who got what and how much. This is still the case, except government has now gotten control of the distribution and unequally distributes that wealth to those who allow them that power that is now codified in laws government was never empowered to enact but ignoring the requirement of uniformity as required by law. In other words, equally distributed.

The constitutions of the individual States and that which binds the federal government contains a provision barring the passage of bills of attainder. That is laws singling out individuals or groups. The Lords of England agreed to fealty to the King of England under the condition he was not to enact laws singling out one or more of them for special treatment, in this case punishment. This provision is embodied in the Magna Carta and was incorporated in the constitutions of the states and the federal government purposely to insure equal treatment under the law. The unequal distribution of the nation's wealth is embodied in what is called the "tax code" that is a succession of laws and regulations constituting the largest collection of bills of attainder ever assembled and now numbering over 70,000 pages and growing.

For nearly a century the United States relied on tariffs on imported goods as a means to obtain revenue. It was not only a source of revenue but enabled the mercantile north to develop its own mercantile economy reducing its reliance on imported manufactured goods, primarily from England. It also placed an unequal burden on the southern States that were primarily still in the agricultural economy and purchased manufactured goods in exchange for their agricultural output, mainly cotton and tobacco rather than from the northern mercantile States where it was more expensive. The southern States were therefore paying the bulk of the federal budget. The South, becoming less powerful politically due to the addition of new States entering the Union. These States had little reliance on imports and therefore made them neutral or favorable to the status quo. The growing political schism and the South's inability to rectify the situation legally through changing the tax laws would ultimately result in the Civil War and the attempt by the South to unleash the burden of taxation. That same schism today exists between the owners of nature's assets and those who must work for them and is being mollified politically by borrowing to finance the welfare state.

Addendum

America prides itself on being a nation of laws. Is it because we have more laws than any other nation on the planet? No. Although true that we do have more laws than anyone else it is because we have more people who obey those laws? Doubtful, because China has almost 3 billion people and India over 1 billion making it highly probable that they have more people obeying their laws than we do. What we can take pride in is the fact that nature has blessed America with an abundance of what is necessary to sustain human life and despite the very fact that our politicians have broken nearly every law they designed to afford us the right to life, liberty and the pursuit of happiness, we still can. An explanation is necessary to clarify the last statement.

The Ten Commandments were the law set down to Moses in the old testament and the regulations contained in the book of Leviticus that form the Torah or body of Jewish law. Other than the ones relating to having no other God and honoring your parents the remainder of the law relates to stealing and the regulations on how to live one's life and honor their Lord. These apply to all Christians, Jews and to Muslims and are covered by reference in the Qur'an. So long as nature produces sufficient fuel (food) to sustain life and theft is punished man will survive. If the regulations are observed, that life will be tranquil.

When man formed tribes and societies but was still nomadic, self-governance was satisfactory because there was little to steal except for food and since it was shared the need for theft only occurred if there was not enough to go around and even then, those who hunted and fished were assured an adequate share before the rest had to share what was left. When man learned to cultivate his food and multiplied beyond the need or ability for each to produce his own sharing ceased and ownership of nature's assets where those who owned them could determine who got how much of what barter replaced sharing. As the population multiplied many had only their time to barter and a means of exchange had to be introduced to value that time.

The industrial revolution, coupled with the continuing increase in population reduced the ability of many to sell their time. The consequence was the migration of those of the population who could retreat to places where this cycle had yet escaped the industrial revolution. That situation continues today and instead of reducing our population, the owners of nature's assets have now resorted to charity to maintain their ownership but in the process, exacerbate the problem by encouraging the production of an even greater population because it is those who require charity who have the most offspring. They accomplish this feat through government and it will ultimately result in the acceleration of the demise of the human race.

The answer is that it is a false pride to say we are a nation of laws because nearly all of the problems we face as individuals and a society are the result of our elected representatives, who are mostly lawyers, breaking the very law they contrived to govern us. It begins with the State constitutions wherein the State is given the power by the people to defend their lives, their liberties and their property. That is to keep others, including themselves from stealing their lives and property and infringing on their liberties. It is the police power that people surrender in constituting government and to fund the execution of that power agree that the government may tax them to pay for the exercising of that power. In the State of Maine, the government must tax to pay for the services it provides to the public. The laws of economics require that the books balance at the end of the fiscal year and since the governments outlays proceed its income it is authorized to borrow until the tax revenue offsets the expenditure. These are normally called tax anticipation bonds" and are paid as revenue is received to offset them. The State could just as easily collect more in taxes over a period of years to avoid the bank fees on the bonds but that would not be very good for the banks and as you will deduce at the end of this set of revelations it is the banks that control natures assets and insure that their lackeys in the legislatures and in Congress do not rock their boat.

This introductory revelation shows that the very first power and the laws that it requires, that of taxation, have not been upheld as required by oath of the very politicians who have sworn to do so.

Chapter 2
Electing a President

It was my intent to follow up the first chapter with a continuation of the start which began by addressing the powers of the Congress as stipulated in Article 1 Section 8. The recent election took precedence over my intent to follow the outline with which I started that was to go down the various powers given to the Congress as they appear in the document but the fiasco that was the election prompted me to interrupt the sequence since we were confronted with an actual event that illustrated the object of this expose' better than I could do with prose.

"Each State shall appoint, in such manner as the legislature thereof may direct, a number of electors, equal to the whole number of Senators and Representatives to which the State may be entitled in the Congress; but no Senator or Representative, or person holding an office of trust or profit under the United States, shall be appointed an elector.

The electors shall meet in their respective States and vote by ballot for two persons, of whom one at least shall not be an inhabitant of the same State with themselves. And they shall make a list of all the persons voted for and of the number of votes for each; which list they shall sign and certify and transmit sealed to the seat of the government of the United States, directed to the President of the Senate. The President of the Senate shall, in the presence of the Senate and House of Representatives, open all the certificates and the votes shall then be counted. The person having the greatest number of votes shall be the President, if such number be a majority of the whole number of electors appointed; and if there be more than one who have such majority, and have an equal number of votes, then the House of Representatives shall immediately choose by ballot one of the them for President; and if no person has a majority then from the five highest on the list the said House shall in like manner choose the President. But in choosing the President, the votes shall be taken by States, the representation from each State having one vote; a quorum for this purpose shall consist of a member or members from two thirds of the States and a majority of the States shall be necessary to a choice. In every case, after the choice of the President, the person having the greatest number of votes of the electors shall be the Vice President. But if there should remain two or more who have equal votes, the Senate shall choose from them by ballot for Vice President." This system was intended to insure that only one of their own (elected politicians) could be elected.

Evidence of the latter is the provision that one of the qualifications is being born in the United States or attaining the age of 35 and having been a resident for 14 years. It just so happens this latter qualification was made to fit Alexander Hamilton, a delegate, who happened to be born in Jamaica but been resident 14 years in the United States after having attended Yale University. Coincidence? Unlikely.

It seems a very complicated scheme but it is Socratic in its methodology and in essence is the system called "rank choice". The design is to weed out alternatives until a majority can agree on one. The intent of the framers was to select individuals who knew persons who could and be willing to fill the position of President. The reason was that in the late 1780s there was only a small cadre of people who had a national identity and fewer still known outside their States. The framers undoubtedly considered that whoever was to be chosen would be one of their own and designed this system to insure it. That a choice was to made of someone not from one's own State resulted in the coinage of the term "favorite s11 on candidate. Regardless, the system assumed the result would not be predetermined or the vote be by popular ballot of the people.

The system works reasonably well if the number of choices is small but breaks down as the number of choices is increased. In statistics, the choices are reduced to two and as a result conclusions can be drawn from samples of the total number of two alternatives if the choice of the sample is correctly designed. For example, the choice is between a Hershey bar and a Nestle bar. You could not expect Nestle to be chosen if you sampled only people living in Hershey Pennsylvania. A classic example is the selection of the Pope by the College of Cardinals. Italy, for a long period, had a majority of its countrymen in the College of Cardinals the consequence of which the Pope was almost always Italian. It did not mean that among the Italian Cardinals there was unanimity, it just meant that ultimately the choice would be an Italian Cardinal.

As for the United States the inefficiency of this system did not arise until the election of 1800 when two candidates, Thomas Jefferson and Aaron Burr tied and both had a majority of the votes cast because each elector had two votes. One hundred thirty votes were cast for other candidates. The result was the election was decided by the House of Representatives by a vote of 10 States to 4 with 2 abstaining. Thomas Jefferson became President and the runner up Aaron Burr became Vice President, people of opposite political views. It also resulted in the 12th Amendment to the Constitution that separated the election to a vote for President and another for Vice President. This fix did not solve the core problem because the number of electors was increasing with the addition of new States, resulting in an even greater number of favorite sons getting votes reducing the chance of any one getting a majority.

It was not until 1824 that a popular vote was introduced but the electors were not bound by it since it would have been unconstitutional. It so happened that the ultimate winner got 113,122 votes and the loser133,122. In 1836 the Vice President was selected by the Senate. In 1976 one Washington elector voted for Ronald Reagan even though he was not a candidate. In 1988 one West Virginia elector voted for Lloyd Benson for President and Michael Dukakis for Vice President though each candidate was running for the opposite office.

It is obvious that the major parties could have none of the uncertainty that came with this system, in particular having the President be a member of one party and the Vice President a member of another. They also had to put hurdles in the way to prevent a third or fourth party from having a chance to be elected. How did they accomplish this?

The Constitution stipulates that the State legislature may dictate the manner in which the electors are chosen. The Constitution of the State of Maine provides "A vote for the candidate for President is a vote for the presidential electors nominated by the candidate's political party or by petition." Their vote is proscribed as follows;" The presidential electors at large shall cast their ballots for the presidential and vice-presidential candidates who received the largest number of votes in the State. The presidential electors of each congressional district shall cast their ballots for the presidential and vice- presidential candidates who received the largest number of votes in each respective congressional district." In this manner, the loser gets no votes. These quotes are taken from Title 21-A, Chapter 9 sub-chapter 5 of the Maine Constitution.

The Maine legislature took the independence of the vote of the electors out of their hands and placed it in the hands of the political parties recognized by the State of which there was initially only two. It also had to eliminate the vote of the electors. The way this now works is the parties are given the power to choose the electors and the electors are bound to vote for the candidate chosen by the party. In 2016 the electors chosen by the people for the Republicans is Donald Trump and for the Democrats Hillary Clinton. They will not actually follow the proscribed constitutional method. I do not know how the Electors of the State of Maine are chosen or whether they actually vote or not. Maine has four electoral votes and the winner of those votes is determined by the results of the popular vote and even if 49% voted for a different candidate it is if their vote did not count. It is why the majority of the framers decried democracy because it a way for 51% to subjugate the other 49%.

When you vote in your party's primary it is the only time you have a free choice but you can only vote for whom the party has deemed electable in a general election or waste your vote on a write-in. In a general election, you get a choice of either of the two-party's candidate or a write-in. If you do not have party leanings you do have the option of voting for a candidate not of either party but whoever is running as an independent. As with write-in candidates it is like entering a lawn tractor in the Indy-500.

Conclusion

The framers originally designed a system to select the President and Vice President that was doomed to result in the inability to select a winner on the first round and result in a plethora of ballots before a victor emerged and therefor unworkable. In

recognition of this they adopted the 12th Amendment to the Constitution that did not solve the problem because they failed to realize that although the number of votes was limited, the potential candidate pool was not. The political parties, of which there have only been two of consequence have solved that problem by limiting the number of candidates who are now chosen on the basis of popularity as opposed to competence. How do you become popular, you promise people something for their vote? Initially it was patronage jobs and the absence of regulation and when the parties found they could raid the treasury with impunity it became pure charity and favoritism as regards regulation.

Yes, Bob and Jane, you too can become the President of the United States but, first you will have to become a member of either the Republican or Democrat Party. You need not be competent so long as you are popular. You will have to learn to lie with a straight face, avoid any exposure of unacceptable conduct, smile convincingly and be able to tell people you will give them more than they already have and won't take what they have away. If you are blessed with a Congress of the same party, you may even be able to keep your promises.

Chapter 3
Duties of the President

Article II of the U. S. Constitution sets out the method of selecting the President and defining his duties and powers. The manner of election was covered in Chapter 2 of the series written at the time of the recent election. This chapter will concentrate on the duties, responsibilities and powers of the President and Vice President.

"Before he enters on the Execution of his Office, he shall take the following oath or affirmation: - "I do solemnly swear (or affirm) that I will faithfully execute the Office of President of the United States, and will to the best of my ability, preserve, protect and defend the Constitution of the United States". This is the oath of office required of every President and any Vice President rising to the office for whatever reason. Other elected members of the Congress and the Vice President take a similar but significantly different oath, as proscribed in one of the first laws passed by the Congress. It reads, *""I, a Representative of the United States in the Congress thereof, do solemnly swear or affirm (as the case may be) that I will support the Constitution of the United States. "*(italics added)

The Vice President is the head of the Senate and hence a member of the Congress. The procedure is for Vice President to administer the oath to the members of Congress and then one of these sworn members administers the oath to the Vice President. Should he be elevated to the office of the President he is required to take the oath as stipulated for the significant difference in their responsibilities is one of defending the Constitution, not just supporting it. It is the veto power that enables the President to "defend" the Constitution from assault by the Congress. It is the power misused by George Washington in signing the National Bank Act and ultimately taken away in the decision by Chief Justice Marshall in his opinion in the case of McCulloch vs. Maryland (19 US 316) in 1819. This power, although specifically intended to stem the overreach of the Congress despite the rise of political parties aligned along economic lines, is sterile when the Congress is composed of a majority of one party the same as that of the President. It allows that party to do whatever it will.

Power is money and money begets power. You recall the golden rule, he who has the money makes the rules. The economic system that the colonists adopted from their parent England assures the validity of this rule and no civil war or other political upheaval can change it so long as the winning party adopts the same economic system that only rearranges the deck chairs on the Titanic. Totalitarianism, communism, socialism, and fascism are variant economic systems none of which can achieve the balance of a shared system that enables each to share equally the fruits of nature and rewards those who make it work.

Article II Section I states, "the executive power shall be vested in a President of the United Sates of America. *He* (italics added) shall hold *his* (italics added) office during the term of four years and together with the Vice President, chosen for the same term, be elected as follows:" The words he and his have been italicized to reinforce the intent that the framers of the document wanted to make abundantly clear that the elected to these offices would be of the male sex as had been the practice of their predecessors in England under the monarchy and confirmed as set down in the Magna Carta.

The Magna Carta does not stipulate the sex of the monarch but all royal titles traditionally pass down from the father who is recognized as the law giver in the family, whether the family be only two. If the man dies without heir, the title to the land reverted back to the monarch to redistribute according to his will and the title eliminated of given another as determined by the monarch. If the monarch were to die without male heir the title would revert to the brother or his sister's male heir. If the monarch dies intestate or without any male heir the title is then determined by the privy council or Lords of the realm. Under the current parliamentary system of England, the monarch no longer has the power to make law, therefore the head of the political party becomes the Prime Minister and he or she alone cannot make law and it is therefore immaterial as to whether the Prime Minister is a man or woman.

In the case of the Constitution, the President cannot make law, but no law can become such without his concurrence unless it is reenacted by a super majority of the House and Senate. As in the case of ancient England, the King could make law with the restrictions imposed as regards taxes, the framers wanted the law to be enacted and administered by men. In essence, the King was the President, the Senate the House of Lords and the House of Representatives the Parliament. The original Virginia Constitution of 1776, that was the frame work for the Constitution of the United States is gender specific as regards both the House of Burgesses and their House of Delegates including the office of governor. The gender specific wording of the U. S. Constitution only applies to the President and Vice President but it is clear from precedent, both in the government of England at the time and the States that public office was the purview of men. The confirmation of this is that women were only given the privilege of voting in federal elections in 1920 and that privilege did not extend to the privilege of holding federal office.

It was not because Thomas Jefferson, actually parroting comments made by his friend George Mason, penned in the Declaration that all men were equal that women were held in second place. On the contrary, their contribution to family life made them every bit the equal of the man in the house but, one had to be the law (rule) maker and tradition has extended that role to men. The words of Mason that he omitted were "under the law". They were significant in that they began the breakdown of the family and the removal of the main responsibilities of mothers, the education of the children until the boys were ready to undertake the tutelage of their father and the girls ready to assume the same responsibilities as their mothers. It was Thomas Jefferson, the deist, who promoted the establishment by the government of public education in order to remove the influence of the Church of England but to remove the teaching of its dogma. It is a similar reason the Progressives want to get control of the American school system and that is to teach their brand of dogma.

Section 2 states the "President shall be Commander in Chief of the army, and navy of the United States and of the militia of the several States, when called into the actual service of the United States". The calling into action relates to the power given only to the Congress to declare war. Like the States, the President could not function in this regard on his own "unless actually invaded, or in such imminent danger as will not admit of delay". The delay being the time to call the Congress together to vote to go to war.

We have been invaded on only three occasions; by the British in 1812, by Mexico in 1846 in an effort to retrieve the Republic of Texas that Texans had seized from Mexico and later annexed by the United States and the attack by Japan in 1941 on Pearl Harbor, at that time a territory of the United States. The federal government had been at war with various Indian tribes almost continually since the establishment of the first colonies in the 1600s. It ended only in the late 1800s and the animosity has been relegated to non-armed conflict that, like the Civil War, continues between the parties to this day.

War is armed robbery in that in order to obtain something someone has but does not want to voluntarily give it up. A contract or treaty on the other hand is an agreement to cede something you have in surplus or willing to trade for something the other has that you want and he similarly considers it surplus or non-essential in order to obtain what you are offering in exchange. When you can agree, they are of equal value to you the exchange is made.

Chapter 4
Naturalization and Bankruptcy

Article 1 Section 8 gives the Congress the power "To establish a uniform rule of naturalization and uniform laws on the subject of bankruptcies throughout the United Sates". Words mean things. There is nothing so clear as to the intent of the framers that the federal authority makes the rules for certain elements common to all the States to insure uniformity. They did not give the federal authority the power to determine who is eligible under the rules. That power belonged to the States. The truth of this interpretation is evident in the first paragraph of Article 1 Section 9 which states," The migration or importation of such persons as any of the States now existing shall think proper to admit, shall not be prohibited by the Congress prior to the year 1808, but a tax or duty may be imposed on such importation.

Portions of this clause were aimed strictly at the slave trade and the compromise made to the southern States in order to get their agreement to the whole. The key phrase is "shall not be prohibited". The Congress had the option after 1808 to prohibit immigration but not to foster it. That power was retained by the States as evidenced by the phrase "as any of the States now existing shall think proper to admit".

As with any compromise, it usually creates more problems than it solves. They began when the country was expanding and new States were being admitted to the Union. They did not fall into the category "now existing" and therefore the Congress' could not prohibit the introduction of slavery because it had no power over the territories once they were admitted as States. Since the northern or mercantile states had the majority in the government they compromised with the slave holding states the result of which was the Missouri Compromise of 1850. In the same year the Congress passed the separate but complimentary Fugitive Slave Act that required the States to return fugitive slaves to their owners. The slave states avoided the prohibition of slavery by agreeing that Utah and New Mexico Territories would not admit slaves unless they wanted to and California was admitted as a free state. The slave states did not really gain anything as neither Utah nor New Mexico was suited to plantation agriculture requiring an abundance of cheap (indentured) labor.

The economics of slave labor and the laws necessary to perpetuate it are beyond the scope of this discussion, save to say it was the basis for the disagreement between the North and the South regarding States rights that led to the Civil War.

The words, "now existing" give rise to the reason for their inclusion. The only rational explanation can be better explained if one replaces the word States with Tribes. Each of the 13 original colonies were founded primarily by Englishmen of various religious persuasions with the exception of New York that had already morphed to a similar one as the others although originally settled by the Dutch. It was the framer's intent therefore to restrain the expansion to the west to natural growth of these tribes or their members who had remained behind in their former country. It was never intended as a haven for those oppressed in their own countries by dictators or a majority with dissimilar beliefs.

That the country is able to absorb the numbers of people beyond those intended by the framers is a testament to the farmers and agricultural development of the nation that has expanded the yield of renewable food supplies to their very limits. That limit has been reached but our economic system has skewed its production such that the number of energy units necessary to sustain life has been decreasing while the demand for more units is increasing. Because the distribution of these units is controlled by the government it favors those who give it the power to skew this distribution. Deterioration of the total units per person began decreasing in the mid1980s and continues unabated. Had the government not subsidized nearly all unit production, the slide would be even worse. The continued absorption of refugees and illegal migration through our southern border only exacerbates the situation.

It should be mentioned here that in agreeing to treaties between nations one of the conditions must be that each party is obligated to take back any of its citizens the other has not invited by the issuance of a visitor's visa or work or residence permit and any who on applying for naturalization fail to meet the countries requirements.

Bankruptcy occurs when income is insufficient to cover expenses. At this point a firm or individual can declare itself unable to take action to reverse the condition or must liquidate its assets in order to pay the creditors. In some states, an individual's home is protected from liquidation to pay debt in a bankruptcy. Those who rent are not protected and if they go bankrupt because of lack of income they then must survive through private charity or government largess.

The economic system and the distribution system is now controlled by the government, through the Federal Reserve. The competitive nature of the system creates compensable income only if the employer can recover its cost from the sale of its product or service. The mercantile economy is built primarily on the utilization of earth's non- reproducible assets and to attract the manpower necessary is forced to pay an amount necessary to attract those living on the agricultural and barter economy. The least expensive would be adult males or females with no dependents.

Coupled with the production of more uncompensated workers and dependents were government policies that encouraged the production of more uncompensated workers through private and government subsidized welfare and labor laws that established hours, required extra compensation for overtime work, mandated a minimum wage and with the opportunity for organized labor to bargain with employers collectively essentially gave it the license to extort money from their employer. This was initially protected by tariffs on imported manufactured goods and resulted in price inflation making the domestic product more expensive than imports. When employers could no longer recover the cost due to foreign competition manufacturers continued to employ labor saving methods and where they could they moved the jobs overseas to countries where they could employ cheaper labor. Where they could not the jobs went to foreign employers.

The laws passed by the Congress and then the States in regard to labor were laws and regulations actually prohibited to the States and never given to the Congress by their respective constitutions. In truth, State constitutions and the federal constitution prohibit the States from "impairing the obligations of contracts". The selling of one's labor for compensation is a contract. In addition, these laws contain exceptions and exclusions which in itself makes them "bills of attainder" or laws or regulations applicable only to certain individuals or groups and hence unconstitutional (illegal).

If it were not for government welfare, direct government employment, firms whose only customer is government (military industrial complex) or subsidized employers a large portion of employable workers without jobs would swell even faster than it has. The tipping point will come when the money being distributed through welfare will be insufficient to cover the cost of food and other essentials. A system whereby politicians determine who gets how much of nature's bounty and favor those who give them that power will fail because those left out will ultimately resort to theft either individually or in mass. It is what is happening in Africa and the middle east.

Chapter 5
Coinage and the Value of Money

Article 1 Section 8 of the U. S. Constitution contains a paragraph wherein the Congress is given the power "To coin money, regulate the value thereof and of foreign coin and fix the standards of weights and measures". The framers of the Constitution had the opportunity to introduce an economic system that reflected the fact that the world's non-reproducible assets are finite and its reproducible assets are limited by the amount of arable land and water necessary for its reproduction. Instead they adopted the British system from which they came that required man to work to obtain the exchange needed to insure his survival. The British in turn adopted this system from prior governments and was based on the ownership of nature's assets. Ownership of nature's assets meant that the owners could then determine their distribution. A system that requires one to work for their survival ignores the fact that children cannot produce useful work and the elderly cannot compete with more youthful adults for the jobs offering exchange for labor. Such a system is doomed to ultimate failure when the mouths to be fed consume the entire food supply necessary to sustain life. The inevitable is only prolonged by government welfare.

The U. S. mint was established by the coinage act of 1792 that established the silver content of the currency and anyone with the metal could have it converted to coinage which was deemed legal for all trade. The States had heretofore produced their own currency in several forms and is an interesting history in its own but beyond the scope of this paper. The intent of the framers of the Constitution was to establish a standard of value that would be the same in all the States (colonies). The mistake they made was to tie its value to a metal whose value was not constant but depended on the cost of its production that is variable.

The only economic system that will sustain human life is based on the fuel value of the foods being produced that sustain life and allow it to produce useful work in order to produce the needs and wants of its members. You cannot drive a car unless you put fuel in the tank nor can you sustain life unless you provide it the means to obtain the fuel necessary to sustain it and produce useful work. This system is described in more detail in my book "The Real Economy" and includes the rules necessary for its efficient functioning. Unlike the U. S. Dollar that accumulates with each new issue thereby diluting the value of those previously issued, the new currency, based on the kcal is consumed each year and replenished the following year provided the society using it produces the requisite number of kcal necessary to sustain life. It is distributed each year in the form of exchange that is consumed as it is used. Those who can perform work can earn some of that distributed to those who do not, thereby improving their lifestyle and providing the incentive to create a family and reproduce, thereby continuing the human race.

The U. S. Dollar has been depreciating at an average rate of 3% per year since 1914, about the same time as the cost to produce an ounce of gold exceeded its imputed value. It now takes about $23.39 to buy what $1.00 did in 1914. This figure is not mine but those of your own government. This is the consequence of an exchange that is not consumed but accumulates. The United States reached its peak production of kcal in the mid-1980s. Even this level of production has to be subsidized by the government that has been subsidizing much of our agricultural (kcal) production since the Great Depression when the wheat crop fell by over 40% in less than 2 years. The United States still produces more kcal than it consumes and exports enough to feed millions more. Those millions more are gradually moving to the United States, legally and illegally, because of their own nation's skewed distribution of their own wealth, agriculturally or otherwise.

It is difficult to predict when the system will fail because it is in different stages in different countries (societies) based on the distribution systems prevalent. In some countries, this distribution system results in open revolt (civil war) depending on the numbers being exploited. In others, it fosters migration to countries where jobs are available or a welfare state exists. The United States is one of the latter. The numbers being exploited and dependent on the welfare system is growing at an alarming rate such that over 44 million are now on food stamps and millions more on other forms of welfare. This even includes some members of the military.

The system does not provide a means for those dependent to rise from their dependent state but as the saying goes, "idle hands breed mischief" and the rise in drug use is but one result of an unequal distribution system. The rise in the number of homeless or malnourished are signs of a welfare system gone awry. Just ask yourself, if the U. S. government stopped distributing welfare in the form of EBT cards, Social Security payments and the like, what would people do to survive? Your only answer is theft in the form of civil war. When the framers decided to adopt this system, they automatically doomed the government to ultimate failure.

The fixing of the standards and of weights and measures is again an attempt to establish a common system throughout the country. This is necessary to insure fair and honest dealing. The United States refused to go along with the rest of the world when it officially adopted the metric system and as a consequence commerce between countries with different systems essentially stifled both imports and exports. Firms whose production demands a standard weight and measurement system have been gradually shifting to it and it has officially been recognized by the

24

government but its adoption has not been mandated. The Metric System of weights and measures will eventually be adopted but the export commerce lost by clinging to the English System will never be recovered.

Chapter 6
Post offices and Post Roads

Article 1 Section 8 of the U. S. Constitution gives the Congress power to: "establish Post Offices and post Roads". This is an extension of the power of a government to take private property for public purposes in order for people to move about unhindered by the ability of property owners to deny access to or transit through their property. Its purpose was to foster communication between persons of the various states when the only mode of communication was the written word or physical presence. The State governments had the responsibility to provide this capability to its own citizens.

This power as far as communication has become unnecessary with the advent of the telephone, radio, the internet and private augmenters for package and mail delivery systems. The obligation for post roads was satisfied by the Interstate Highway system undertaken during the administration of Dwight Eisenhower. The responsibility for maintenance and repair of this system is now the responsibility of the State that the highway serves.

The construction and maintenance of these systems should be borne by those who benefit from them through taxes on fuel, automobiles and trucks.

Because of our economic system the cost in dollars for construction and maintenance continues to rise but taxes and have not been raised accordingly, leading to poorly maintained facilities and the reluctance for new construction. The situation will continue to worsen unless a new economic system is employed.

The budgets of both the states and the federal government were to be balanced by the very constitutions that established them. The means to balance them was provided by the authority to tax to pay for the expense and the ability to borrow against future tax income until it is collected in the year it is spent.

In addition, the governments, both federal and state, have allowed unions or its own employees to extort higher wages and benefits unavailable in the private sector that is not unionized. The federal government funds up to 80% of state highways while not having the power to do so and with money gleaned from taxes and most usually borrowed (printed) and uses these grants to perpetuate the Congressmen and Senators that support it.

Chapter 7
Patents and Copyrights

Article 1 Section 8 of the U. S. Constitution gives the Congress the power to: "promote the progress of science and useful arts, by securing for limited times to authors and inventors the exclusive right to their respective writings and discoveries". This provision is a carry-over from British law that was intended to preserve intellectual property rights. The efficacy of such protection for commercial purposes is questionable since it would be impossible to enforce, particularly in countries where no such protection is afforded. If it extended only to attribution or recognition of individual discovery or production without any commercial impact it would still allow the individual the benefits of being first in the marketplace.

Unfortunately, this provision, particularly with regard to patents, has enabled those holding the patent the monopoly power to exploit their discoveries in some cases for up to 17 years resulting in society paying more for the discovery than would be the case if such power were not exercised.

Not satisfied with the limitations imposed by this provision, the Congress has taken to funding research and development, particularly at universities, where it subsidizes all forms of research thereby obtaining the support of at least the university hierarchy and the researchers for a continuance of this benevolence at taxpayer expense. It has fostered the creation of the National Endowment for the Arts, the National Science Foundation and the Center for Disease Control all of whom are noble institutions but, beyond the power of the Congress to create. These organizations dole out taxpayer funds with the sole purpose of obtaining the votes of those disbursing the funds or their benefactor. The proof is that the budgets of these organizations must be approved each year by those authorizing the disbursement.

Chapter 8
The Courts

Article 1 Section 8 reads, the Congress has the power "to constitute tribunals inferior to the Supreme Court". The responsibilities and authorities of the Supreme Court are covered by Article III of the Constitution and will be covered by a separate chapter. The Congress reserved to itself the power to create subordinate bodies in order to not inconvenience disputants from the origin of the disputing parties. In the late 1700s transportation and communication even within the States was still rather primitive.

The inclusion of the word "inferior" is significant in that it automatically reduced the status of the Supreme Court, based in the capital city (originally Philadelphia) to that of an appellate court. To see how this has been employed by a Justice Department's not following the law one needs only cite the case of the Affordable Care Act (Obamacare).

Contrary to this requirement, the Justice Department remanded and the Supreme Court acquiesced in adjudicating the dispute to a lower court and denying the plaintive States the opportunity to stop its implementation. They did this knowing full well that by the time the case came to the Supreme Court its destructive effects on current health insurance policy holders could not be easily reversed. The court, in defense of its earlier refusal to exert its authority had to find a way to legitimize Congress' action and called the law a tax, a fact that even the Administration that actually wrote the law did not consider. The fact that Congress can only tax to "provide for the common defense and general welfare of the United States" was totally ignored.

Several States objected to the proposed passage of the law as being beyond the purview of the Congress. In its charter (Article III) the Supreme Court has original jurisdiction "In all cases affecting Ambassadors, other pubic ministers and consuls, and those in which a State shall be Party, the Supreme Court shall have original jurisdiction". These words and the reason for them is explained by Hamilton in Federalist 81.

The Supreme Court should have also been given appellate authority in disputes arising between a citizen of a State and his own State. This would have allowed consideration by a federal tribunal in cases where a citizen considered himself improperly treated in comparison to other citizens in similar circumstances or unjustly compensated for claims against the State. In this case sovereignty, did not mean the State itself was above the law but, could sue and be sued. This obligation is passed down to subdivisions of the State, such as Maine, when it incorporates towns and delegates its police power to its town government.

Chapter 9
Piracy and the Law of Nations

Article 1 Section 8 reads, the Congress has the power "to define and punish piracies and felonies committed on the high seas, and offences against the law of nations". The framers of the Constitution gave recognition to the extra-territorial nature of crimes committed by persons outside the jurisdiction of the individual States. It is also recognition of the fact the federal government has no jurisdiction over the people of the States but, only acts of the States that have an effect on other States.

It may surprise many that piracy still exists and in some cases, is still unpunished in many countries. Somalia is a case in point as is Malaysia and the Philippines. Granted that some efforts are made in the latter two countries, but the piracy still goes on. The main reason is that certain countries, Somalia in particular provide haven for their pirates or are powerless to arrest and punish them.

The Barbary Wars were events involving the United States and particularly Tripoli where pirates were given haven in order to loot American vessels, steal their cargoes and impress their crews. Both Thomas Jefferson and James Madison sent American warships to the harbors from which the pirates operated and ordered their government to cease and desist or be bombarded. Fearing the Americans would do just that they finally agreed to no longer prey on American shipping. Would the same threat yield the same result today? The answer is a resounding no because countries harboring the pirates go unpunished or are not even threatened with punishment.

Chapter 10
War

Article 1 Section 8 reads, the Congress has the power "to declare war, grant letters of marque and reprisal, and make rules concerning captures on land and water". Webster defines war as an armed conflict between nations or between factions in the same nation (civil war). It is interesting that both John Jay and Alexander Hamilton in some of their Federalist papers define the reasons for war and both relate to theft either by one Nation against another of land it claims as its own or within a nation by one faction who claim the opposing faction is stealing their share of nature's assets.

At the end of the Revolutionary War the United States negotiated the Treaty of Paris in which England ceded its claim to territory in America. This made the United States collectively a very large landowner of lands that did not already belong to the individual colonies (States). The land claims of the States in many cases such as Virginia and Pennsylvania were unclear and not well defined. Most of the what was then the United States had not been surveyed and boundaries subject to dispute. There was a real fear that England would again try to regain their dominion of the United States and that when the new federal government created new States from the unsold territory ceded by England the States, such as Virginia who claimed, by reason of a grant from the English King, the land from "sea to sea". Such disputes were previously settled by war, but were averted by inclusion of settlement of disputes between states by a Supreme Court of the United States whose decisions were acknowledged as final under the Constitution agreed to by the original States and as a condition of entry of new States. At the time of the Revolution nearly all of North America was claimed by either England, France or Spain.

There remained one more dispute between States that could lead to war and that was where one State could use its economic power to disadvantage that of a neighboring State. This was taking the form of duties and tariffs imposed on goods surplus to one state and sold at a higher price than paid by its own citizens to that of another that needed or wanted the surplus. It was also evident in tariffs charged by States who possessed seaports for goods passing through those States to other States. This probable cause for war was taken care of by the prohibitions of such actions in Article I Section 9 of the Constitution to which all States agreed.

That still leaves the United States with the ability to declare war but has it ever exercised this power? The individual States had been at war with various tribes of Indians who would not recognize the claims of settlers who claimed ownership under land grants from the King of England. These individual wars were ultimately taken over by the federal government who administered the territories until they became States.

The answer is on five occasions and against 10 different countries. In none of these "wars" has the reasons cited by Jay and Hamilton been a factor with two exceptions, that being the War of 1812 to prevent the reversal of the land settlement agreed to by England in the Treaty of Paris. In simple terms, it was an abrogation of the Treaty of Paris. The other was the Civil War where the seceding States were taking land collectively owned by the States as a union.

The second so called war was the Mexican American War of 1846. Texas was a part of Mexico and with their independence from Spain in 1821, Mexico encouraged the settlement of the territory and by 1836 the area was predominately American and German settlers who fought and won independence from Mexico

34

and agreed to statehood in 1845. They tried to take it back and in 1846 James Polk who saw America on a grand scale from coast to coast persuaded the Congress to declare war. It not only saved Texas but in the process Mexico agreed to the ceding of its claims to what was to become Arizona, New Mexico and California with the border now recognized as the Rio Grande River. What started as a war to retain the State of Texas, ended up with a windfall of land the Mexicans knew they could not defend. It was soon to be repeated.

The Spanish American War was a result of our support of Cuban rebels for independence from Spain. When the USS Maine was mysteriously sunk in Havana Harbor the outcry resulted in the ten-week war which saw the United States gain control of Puerto Rico, Guam and the Philippines. Later research of the incident that prompted the conflict indicated the explosion was more likely caused by a coal dust explosion rather than sabotage. Our objective in this "war" was not the acquisition of land because we did not include the acquisition of Cuba. However, to the victor go the spoils and Spain was happy to rid itself of land it could not hold but had to support.

World War I, which is a misnomer in itself, was concentrated in Western Europe, in particular France, The Netherlands, Belgium and Western Germany, but involved Great Britain due to its treaties with others of the belligerents. The United States had no stake in the game other than it aided Great Britain with economic and military aid. Sentiment against Germany was roused by the sinking of HMS Lusitania with the loss of over 1700 lives that President Woodrow Wilson succeeded in obtaining a declaration of war against Germany on April 6, 1917 and its ally Austria-Hungary on December 7, 1917. We had become the suppliers of mercenaries for the first time in someone else's war.

We are not even good mercenaries. A mercenary is a soldier of another country paid to fight the enemy of its hirer. The practice was common in Europe where one ruler would rent his army to another. We on the other hand lend our army for free and prohibit them from taking the spoils of war and on top of it pay for the damage we cause. We also expose our troops by tying their hands with rules in a conflict where the only rule is kill or be killed. Much of the supplies will sell to the combatants we support are never paid for. The Soviet Union in the case of World War II is a classic example. This same practice is applied in peace time through organizations such as the World Bank and A. I. D. This enriches the banks and when countries default or the government forgives the loans the taxpayers foot the bill for the loss because the banks are protected by government guarantee of their loan amount.

On December 7, 1941, the Japanese navy attacked our Pacific fleet in Pearl Harbor for the sole purpose of preventing it from coming to the aid of the counties it was at war with in the Pacific of which our territories of the Philippines and Guam were included. Had we given them their independence like Spain did with Cuba we had no justification to declare war and should have sued for damages instead. We were already helping the Chinese in their defense of their country against the Japanese. We lost the defensive war but regrouped and ultimately won the offensive war and drove out the Japanese invader. The big mistake was President Franklin Roosevelt also got the congress to declare war against Germany on December 11, 1941 and against Germany's allies, Bulgaria, Hungary and Romania on June 5, 1942. As in World War I Germany's beef against the United States was that we were openly aiding their enemy.

We are now fighting a war against an enemy whose only beef with us is that we overtly come to the aid of their enemies the government that subjugates them. To claim they have designs on invading the United States lacks credibility. These are civil wars being fought by factions within their own countries because they are being denied their share of their countries assets, either because they are of a different tribe than the leaders, harbor a different religion or are of a different political philosophy. Our country is not at risk. We have not been attacked with the purpose of obtaining our land or killing all of our people or ejecting them from our land. Therefore, the Congress, nor the President has the authority to act against these so-called terrorists because they are only trying to get us to mind our own business. Like the Spanish have done after the Madrid Rail bombing, if we as a nation accede to the demand to cease helping those who are oppressing them, they will stop. It is not cowardice to retreat from a conflict you have no business in but an acknowledgment or error.

President Dwight Eisenhower cautioned the nation of the avarice of the so called "Military Industrial Complex" whose existence and profits depend on a constant state of war or war readiness. We have failed to heed his warning and their lobbyists have succeeded in convincing enough politicians that war and military readiness are in the nation's best interest. None of the billions spent on preparation to defend our country goes to prevent the foreign invasion which is now under way in an entirely different way with the invasion of millions of Mexicans and Latin Americans occupying our land and the Chinese buying it with our own money.

Letters of Marque and Reprisal are now an antiquated system to legalize piracy. Privateers once roamed the seas preying on merchant vessels of other countries. They were given license to so they would not be prosecuted for piracy on the high seas by the country issuing the Marque. The practice was stopped with the advent of International Law conventions but only for countries who accede to the conventions.

Conclusion:

War, as defined is the acquisition of land or the retrieval of land once owned and is undertaken for the sole purpose of insuring your citizens have enough food for survival. Wars, even civil wars become necessary because the economic system adopted by governments unfairly distributes nature's wealth to those who enable them that power. When this wealth takes the form of the food supply and becomes insufficient to both sate the appetites of the majority and the minority it is the minority who must relinquish their meager share. This situation existed in Ireland at the time of the "Potato Famine of the 1800s. The same was the case of Midwestern farmers during the dust bowl of the early 1930s so aptly chronicled by Steinbeck in his "Grapes of Wrath".

We are now providing mercenaries to various factions whose governments have been denying their share of their country's wealth. When and if they succeed in overturning the government they will impose the same system on those they defeated and the process will continue to repeat itself. We have averted this condition to some extent by adopting a welfare system that at least assures the vast majority of those who cannot work and earn a living to survive. Few miss out on this largess and are helped by private charity. The problem is their numbers are growing and our politicians want to accept more fleeing other countries to get in on what they cannot get in their own country. Our politicians, of both parties fight over these forever dependent immigrants for votes while at the same time subsidize the production or more indigenously. The saying that you cannot have your cake and eat it too is a falsehood until you run out of flour.

Chapter 11
Raising Armies

Article 1 Section 8 reads, the Congress has the power "to raise and support armies, but no appropriation of money to that use shall be for a longer term than two years." This power is complemented by a further power "to provide for calling forth the militia to execute the laws of the Union, suppress insurrections and to repel invasions". The framers feared what they left in England and that was a king with a private army that in addition to warring against foreign countries he could use it to quell rebellion within by citizens opposed to his policies. At the time of the establishment of the United States, the Confederation was at war at war with various Indian Tribes. In order to remove the natives from land this responsibility fell initially to the British army then the responsibility fell to the Confederation when war with England was declared. After the Declaration of Independence these wars were assumed by the federal government because it was land owned collectively by all the States.

The State militias were formed to provide protection of the State from foreign invasion that applied reasonably only to those States that were exposed to this possibility. The federal government was then empowered to be able to mobilize the militias of other States to come to their aid. The militia could be mobilized by the governor to quell internal rebellion. The powers were clarified by the Insurrection Act of 1807 and further clarified by the Posse Comitatus Act of 1878 further amended in 2006.

The Insurrection Act, contrary to popular opinion, does not prohibit the federal government to call forth troops or the militias to quell lawlessness within the country or the States. It only sets the requirements under which the federal government can take action. Initially it was only if the State itself was unable to quell the lawlessness but has been expanded such that the federal government can step in without being requested by a State and not only for the sake of quelling rebellion, but to prevent theft of property.

The invasion by illegal aliens is a case in point. The federal government usurped the power of the original 13 States to admit to the country whomever they chose and reserved only to itself the power to stop immigration in total. It all revolved around the meaning of the term "now existing" as included in Article 1 Section 9 of the Constitution as regards the importation of persons. The States would interpret this to mean not only the original 13 States but each State as it were admitted to the Union. The federal government, on the other hand could and did interpret this to mean *only* the original thirteen and that it had the authority to determine how many and what persons were to be admitted. As a consequence, it began establishing quotas under immigration laws that were not challenged by the States. The objective was to control immigration to those who were able to support themselves and not become wards of the Union.

Under pressure from benevolent voters these laws were constantly changed to admit those who would become wards of the Union or who were being persecuted in their own countries. That is by dictators or democratic majorities not sharing their countries wealth equally with all of their citizens. Failure to even enforce these laws has resulted in the ingress of persons fleeing their own countries for similar reasons and the government's failure to stop or even deport them, again under pressure from those who believe they are being benevolent. The federal government has the power to stop this illegal immigration with federal troops to enforce federal law but the States are powerless to intervene because the

States are not empowered to enforce federal law, even if it is unconstitutional. The federal government has chosen not to because of political pressure.

An attempt to rectify this situation was proposed in the Kentucky and Virginia Resolutions of 1798 and 1799 penned by Thomas Jefferson, then Vice President and James Madison respectively. These were passed by the respective legislatures in order to put forth the right that the States had the authority to determine acts of the Congress unconstitutional. Ten northern States refused to agree and the precedent became one of key factors in causes of the Civil War.

The appropriation limit of two years coincided with the terms of the members of the House of Representatives to enable, but not encumber, future representatives if the need for such armies were no longer required. The framers could see that it would take time to populate and secure the country against foreign invaders and that it would be a slow process thereby spreading out its expense. It was done to prevent the establishment of a permanent army that could be used against the people by anyone powerful enough to take over the government such as another State of group of States.

The establishment of two separate bodies to make law was a compromise from the British parliamentary system to which the States had been accustomed wherein the majority party ruled and made law in other words a democracy they so feared. Each colony had its legislature such as the House of Burgesses in Virginia. Virginia adopted a bicameral legislature in its first Constitution in 1776 and it became the model on which the Constitution was based. When the framers met to establish a union among States with varied economic systems those still operating under an agricultural or barter economy could not acquiesce to a government dominated by those operating under a mercantile system that would have resulted in their dominance by the mercantilists of the north, particularly when it came to paying the accumulated debt of the country and future tax burdens. The establishment of two houses based on population including counting of three fourths of the slaves and taxation based on wealth and not per head and the all appropriations of money was the compromise that resulted in a near equality between the south and the north. Unfortunately, most of the States copied this democratic form. It worked until the new States added to the union morphed from agricultural to mercantile economies. The latter was accelerated by the industrial revolution. It was then when one party had control of both houses that an amendment was proposed (XVII) allowing a popular vote for Senators. The mercantilists had succeeded in transforming what was proposed as a Republic to a democracy which it already had become when the Congress started passing legislation directing the people after 1819s decision by the Supreme Court in McCulloch vs. Maryland.

The only thing that keeps the minority of the population from stealing to survive or revolting against those who take the lion's share of the nation's wealth is the welfare state perpetuated by the majority in its own defense through government welfare. They will be able to sustain it only so long as they have the ability to dispense welfare and that will occur when there is insufficient food (fuel) to sustain the inequality of its distribution.

Chapter 12
The Navy

Article 1 Section 8 reads, the Congress has the power "to provide and maintain a navy". The Revolution illustrated to the framers that the federal government could not exercise its obligation under the Constitution to "provide for the defense and general welfare of the States". The words "general welfare" were an unfortunate carryover from the Articles of Confederation. They have been used to institute all sorts of mischief by the Congress that are beyond the scope of this essay. During the Revolution, the Continental Congress had to resort to privateers under Letters of Marque and Reprisal" but was obviously insufficient since there were not many privateers and the British were able to land troops at will. John Paul Jones was one of the first to command a warship under the flag of the Continental Congress and later the flag of the United States.

That the objective of the Congress and hence the federal government was solely defense is clearly illustrated by the limits imposed and the purpose of America's military, now including a Coast Guard, Air Force and Marines that were an adjunct of even our earliest navy as the fighting force on our ships in addition to its crew. It was never intended to be of such strength as to be an offensive force. It has become so to satisfy the needs of what President Dwight Eisenhower, one of our greatest generals, the "military industrial complex", under the so-called guise of defense, has perpetuated this posture with the help of its lobbied Congressmen for its own survival.

The United States has engaged in offensive war on only three occasions; the Revolutionary War in which we engaged the British to retrieve land they claimed and then stole from the Indians, the

Mexican-American War in which we retrieved the state of Texas and acquired land the Mexicans had claimed and had taken back from Spain and World War II in which we took back land from the Japanese that had been initially stolen by Spain from its inhabitants and then ceded to the United States as a result of our retaliatory invasion of Cuba as a consequence of the sinking of our warship the USS Maine in Havana harbor that turned out to be an accident

To add to this sorry record, we have engaged Germany and Italy in WWII as mercenaries as we are now doing openly in the middle east and elsewhere on behalf of legitimate governments and illegitimately with minority factions who seek to overthrow their established governments. Even in this we are inconsistent in that we back the Sunni Muslims in Yemen and the Shiite Muslims against them in Iraq.

The United States has never been invaded for the purpose of securing our land and its agricultural and mineral wealth. The only nations with an opportunity to do so are Canada and Mexico. The Canadians have no interest in doing so as they have enough natural wealth not to risk retaliation or defeat. The Mexicans have already invaded as have many other Latin American countries whose citizens can make it through Mexico or by sea and we have not only failed to stop them but have all but encouraged them to come.

Nuclear weapons are neither offensive or defensive but a show of power by the bully nations. Their use by any nation that possesses them would result in retaliation that even the most insane leader of his nation could not accept. In the hands of terrorist and used in the form of retaliation would likewise bring havoc upon the very group that chose to use them. The reason they are of no use as offensive weapons is that they make the area in which they are used useless to anyone for years due to radiation.

The Swiss have nearly abandoned their Army and air force of course have no navy, but retain a national guard and the semblance of an air force, none of which are supplied with arms from domestic sources. The reason they were not engulfed by Hitler during WWII was simple. The Swiss were prepared and would have inflicted unacceptable casualties and in exchange gained very little because the Swiss were also prepared to initiate a scorched earth policy in the event of a defeat such that the Nazis would have gained nothing for their effort. We should take a lesson from the Swiss.

Chapter 13
Rules of Government

Article 1 Section 8 reads, the Congress has the power "to make rules for the government and regulations of the land and naval forces". Next to its abuse of the regulation of commerce power, this power has allowed the political parties to stifle the enactment of legislation and to thwart the collection of funds to pay the cost of government. Needless to say, if the Congress had adhered to the limitations imposed by the Constitution this power would have been somewhat sterile in its impact. When the limitations on Congressional activity was removed by the McCulloch vs. Maryland decision and Congress could then begin to raid the treasury on behalf of those who gave them the opportunity it became the means for the ruling party to impede and actually stop the opposition party to do the same for its supporters.

None of this would have had any effect if the provisions of Article 1 Section 9 were not also totally ignored. This prohibition states that "no bill of attainder or ex post factor law be passed". This provision is almost a direct extraction from the terms drawn between the Lords of England and the King in the Magna Carta. The Lords most feared being singled out (attained) by the King for punishment of alleged disloyalty or prohibited from acts that were once acceptable or that were not treated as either acceptable or unacceptable. In simple terms, the law had to apply to all the Lords equally and something previous not subject to the law could not then be prohibited. Nearly all of the laws passed by the federal government since 1819, the date of the McCulloch vs. Maryland Decision fall into these two categories of prohibitions. How did we come to this?

Does the saying one hand washes the other come to mind. That is how nearly all legislation is passed. You vote for my bill that favors my constituents and I'll vote for yours, after all it is someone else's money. The entire tax code is made up of bills of attainder. The Volstead Act and even the eighteenth amendment prohibiting the manufacture and distribution of alcohol are prohibited ex post facto laws. The banning of habit forming drugs is yet another example the consequences of which are making the lawlessness of the 1920s look like child's play.

This abuse of power has gotten out of hand but can become considerably worse if it were not for the fact the two factions are often unable to capture both houses of Congress and the Presidency. It has happened once in the 1930s and the Democrats seized the opportunity to pass legislation that was most damaging to the nation's economy and still passed the constitutionality test in the Supreme Court that then also had 9 Democrat appointed justices. The next time this situation occurred, in the early 1990s, the Republicans did not know how to handle this new-found plum, having spent so many years, nearly 40, of being in the minority. The real damage had already been done and the genie could not be forced back into the bottle.

Men and women are not equal. They don't look alike, have equal physical capacities or even features, particularly as regards organs of reproduction. They are both however necessary for the production of progeny and even then, only for specific periods of time. It is for the continuation of the human species that they are endowed with the urge to create progeny and the female only for a brief period each month and for a limited number of years. Males have been known to be able to fertilize the egg of a woman well into their 80s. Only judgement and self-control keeps the mating from producing more progeny than they can support. In order to accomplish this natural law must be modified to define the limits and punish those who exceed them.

Chapter 14
Calling Out the Militia

Article 1 Section 8 reads, the Congress has the power "to provide for calling forth the militia to execute the laws of the Union, suppress insurrection and repel invasions. That this provision exists gives credence to the supposition the framers never intended the Union have a standing army.

The provision was clarified by the Insurrection Act of 1807 to ensure that the President could not act alone without a request from a governor and the approval of the Congress under its unilateral power to declare war. It has been modified several times under Posse Comitatus laws governing the use of the militias (state national guard) and federal troops to enforce domestic policies. As it stands now the President (federal government) is prohibited from using the Army or Air Force to enforce federal law and the states are likewise not empowered to do so. The case in point is enforcement of immigration laws which no President to date has chosen to enforce in the case of illegal immigrants. The States affected are now powerless to act in their defense given the fact they failed to challenge the usurpation by the Congress of the State's ability to determine which persons to admit.

Chapter 15
All Laws Necessary and Proper

Article 1 Section 8 reads, the Congress has the power "to make all laws which shall be necessary and proper for carrying into execution the foregoing powers and all other power vested by this Constitution in the government of the United States, or in any officer or department thereof. The inclusion of this power was necessary to give application to the powers previously enumerated. What has been overlooked or ignored in this power is that it specifically includes only laws not regulations. A law in the strictest sense is the prohibition of a thing. A regulation is the moderation of a legal activity.

Under the Constitution the constituency of the federal government is the States themselves, not the people of those States that are the constituency of that State. The only individuals the federal government has as constituents are counterfeiters of the country's currency, those who commit piracy on the high seas not in possession of a Letter of Marque and Reprisal valid only in the United States and those citizens who commit treason against the country. Individuals as citizens of a State, do not fall within the purview or authority of the federal government unless they fall in the latter categories. That includes bank robbers and persons who flee across State lines to avoid prosecution, persons now strangely under federal authority. The States were given the ability to retrieve indicted criminals from other States that were obligated, if requested, to return them to the State in which their crime was committed. It is the same ability the federal government has in treaties with other countries that contain a clause allowing extradition. It is a useless power to make laws requiring it if there is no consequence for a failure to comply.

It was George Washington who first defied the Constitution's omissions with his acquiescence to Alexander Hamilton's establishment of the first federal corporation, the privately owned National Bank. This was done over the advice of his Secretary of State Thomas Jefferson and his own Attorney General Edmond Randolph.

The attack on the prohibitions of the Constitution came with the passage of the Alien and Sedition Acts. Four laws enacted to modify the laws of naturalization and the federal government's authority to expel or otherwise punish aliens seeking citizenship from countries the United States considered threats to our security or actual enemies. The government, under the Constitution had the power to make rules for naturalization but not the power to expel those who had already become citizens. The real culprit was the law that allowed the government to punish those who spoke against the validity of the law. It was the seed for the Kentucky and Virginia Resolutions. Even though the law was to expire early in the 1800s several people were actually punished under it some even receiving jail time. These were laws passed by the Federalists who, at the time controlled both the Congress and the Presidency. When Thomas Jefferson became President, he pardoned those convicted and reimbursed their fines.

The portion of the Acts punishing sedition expired and were never appealed to the Supreme Court. The Kentucky and Virginia resolutions were never approved by the Federalist Northern States and it was not until the Marbury vs. Madison (5 US 137) did the Supreme Court become the arbiter of constitutionality. They came upon this power not from the Constitution that gives that power to the Executive but by an improperly constructed law of Congress establishing the powers of the Supreme Court. The case and the opinion rendered in it by none other than Chief Justice John Marshall who when given the opportunity in McCulloch vs. Maryland (17 US 317) 12 years later further expanded on the powers of the Congress and the power of the Court, not the President, to be the final arbiter of constitutionality. The mischief this has created, both by the Congress and the Presidency when both are controlled by the same political party has been the sole reason for the acceleration of inflation and the ultimate downfall of the government attempting to reverse it through taxation.

Chapter 16
Making Law

The Articles of Confederation were the initial compact between the States for their mutual protection and general welfare. Article 1 Section 7 outlines the procedure in which a bill becomes law. It reads in part, "every bill which shall have passed the House of Representatives and the Senate, shall, before it becomes a law, be presented to the President of the United Sates; If he approves he shall sign it, but if not he shall return it, with his objections to that house in which it shall have originated, who shall enter the objections at large on their journal and proceed to reconsider it. If after such reconsideration two thirds of that house shall agree to pass the bill, it shall be sent together with the objection, to the other house by which it shall likewise be reconsidered and if approved by two thirds of that house, it shall become a law".

There is an old saying, "follow the money" in search of the cause or solution to any problem. This was certainly the case of the original 13 colonies. All of them were ceded to their founders by the grant of land. They were settled for the potential profits that could be gleaned from the land for the colonists but primarily the King of England through taxes. To protect his investment, the King established the government and stationed his troops to insure compliance to the tax laws and imposts imposed on them by the Parliament. As expected, the new governments adopted the King's economic system that enables government to determine who gets how much of the nation's wealth and the government is established and is made up and perpetuated by those who own that wealth because they were the only ones allowed the vote. To enable this, it is the franchised owners of that wealth who get to perpetuate the system that enables distribution in their favor.

The Articles of Confederation was the mechanism the Colonies, now States, to prosecute the war that would result in wresting the new nation's assets to the control of the State's governments. As the prosecution of the war was the only concern of importance and each was to benefit from attaining that control, actions of the Congress required the approval of each of the States in order for them to be implemented. The Southern, mostly agricultural States, were paying the least of the English taxes on its colonies and it is not surprising the revolt started in the North or mercantile States. They had little to export and relied on imports that were the items most heavily taxed. The non-mercantile south imported less and had its agricultural surplus of cotton and tobacco to generate a large balance of trade. It had less to gain and nothing to lose in wresting control of the country's assets from the British.

This compact to prosecute the war nearly collapsed. You guessed it, it was over who was going to pay for the prosecution of the war. The Continental Congress had no power to tax and could only invoice the States for what was deemed their share of the cost based on the value of their land because it was the same basis used by the Colonies to fund their governments. There was no mechanism to enforce the collection and many States did not pay their share and a few paid nothing. The war eventually cost the Continental Congress $37 million and the States $114 million. At the end of the war, the paper issued by the States and the Continental Congress had virtually no value. The States could retire their debt through taxes but many of them were bankrupt. The Continental Congress had no such power. This situation could have been resolved for future indebtedness by giving the power to tax to the Continental Congress but no mechanism existed in the Articles of Confederation for an entity that would manage and execute the agreement by the States for a common defense. It was for this reason the delegates to the Constitutional Convention decided to create an entirely new agreement. That agreement included the concession that all the States would share the cost accrued by the Continental Congress and the States, but no mechanism was established on how to do it.

The general cost of the new government was estimated to be $3 million per year. The problem, as usual, was to establish some method to raise it while making the burden on the mercantile states roughly equivalent to those of the agricultural states. This was an unachievable task because none of them wanted a pure head tax because it was already the means by which the individual states obtained their own revenue for government. It was particularly true for the slave owning states whose populations were anywhere from 25% to over 50% slave.

	White	Slave	Tax	Per Hd.T	White	Rep.	
1785	000	000	$000			1787	1790
VA	127	293	$513	$1.22	$4.04	16	10
MA	360	0	$449	$1.25	$1.25	14	8
PA	356	4	$410	$1.14	$1.15	13	8
NY	212	21	$256	$1.10	$1.21	8	6
MD	115	103	$283	$1.30	$2.46	9	6
CT	199	3	$264	$1.31	$1.33	8	5
NC	99	101	$218	$1.09	$2.20	7	5
SC	43	107	$192	$1.28	$4.47	6	5
NJ	127	11	$167	$1.21	$1.31	5	4
NH	142	0	$105	$0.74	$0.74	3	3
GA	54	29	$32	$0.39	$0.59	1	3
RI	68	1	$65	$0.94	$0.96	2	1
DE	50	9	$45	$0.76	$0.90	1	1

The first mistake of the framers was to adopt the British parliamentary legislative system of two separate bodies. The framers were not fashioning a government but a confederation to defend the entire country and a mechanism on how to maintain the capability to mobilize it when needed using the resources of each state. As the States were not equal in resources or in the strength of their militias it was an impossible task void of solution if the sovereign states were considered equals. The resultant compromise bore the seeds of its own destruction when the temporary balance they struck came apart with the entry of new States.

The table on the preceding page illustrates the dilemma faced by the Continental Congress prior to the convening of the Continental Congress who were to amend the Articles of Confederation to solve the problem of financing the Revolution. It is evident that if total population were considered as a basis for taxation, that was the basis of the table, the slave holding states would bear the brunt of the tax burden while getting less than half the representation. It was for that reason they did not want a head tax. If only whites were counted the situation was more tolerable but the representation became even worse boding an undesirable future. The situation became tolerable for the moment with the compromise but is likely the reason that delegates like George Mason and two others did not vote for the compromise and championed its rejection in their respective legislatures. The compromise was unanimously approved by the States attending and the negative votes had no impact on their delegation's votes. Rhode Island, the maverick, did not participate and did not vote and was the last to ratify it. It was Benjamin Franklin who opined it was the best they could do under the circumstances and it would suffice for a while and then end in despotism as had all previous others. He acknowledged they had created a government that many of the delegates tried to avoid but were reassured by the federalists among them they had crafted a document that would retain states sovereignty.

It would take less than a year when, at the very first Congress, Alexander Hamilton succeeded in persuading President

Washington to sign into law the establishment of a National Bank against the advice of both his Secretary of State Thomas Jefferson and his Attorney General Edmond Randolph who had been a delegate to the Convention. They said it was not within the power of the Congress to charter corporations and they were right. Hamilton, on the other hand, argued the end justified the means, an argument that would be echoed by Chief Justice John Marshall when he issued the opinion of the Court that the Congress could do almost anything they chose that was not prohibited and took for the Supreme Court the determination of what is constitutional and what is not, usurping the power of the President to reign in the Congress. The case was McCulloch vs. Maryland (17 US 316), itself interesting reading.

The paper the States and the Continental Congress had issued to fund the war had become worthless, but someone was buying it up in anticipation it would somehow be redeemed at full value. The National Bank was a private corporation chartered to collect taxes and pay off the debt assumed by the government from the States as part of the agreement. It was chartered for twenty years and during that period succeeded in redeeming the debt in favor of those who had purchased it at probably 10 cents on the dollar. Whether George Washington himself was a beneficiary of this scheme may never be known. Alexander Hamilton himself was killed in a dual by Aaron Burr.

The seeds of the compromise grew into a poison plant for the southern States and as more States were admitted to the Union, Federalist power grew at the expense of the state's righters and eventually culminated in secession and civil war, Federalist power has become so strong that irrespective of the rise of other political parties they differ now only in the degree of power the federal government should have over the States and their citizens.

Chapter 17
Rules for the Government

Article 1 Section 5 of the United Sates Constitution reads "Each house may determine the rules of its proceedings, punish its members for disorderly behavior and, with the concurrence of two thirds, expel a member". When the Federalists became a clear majority in the Congress and the Supreme Court had taken the lid off restrictions on their efforts to grow the power of the federal government at the expense of the individual States, it was the mechanism they used to impose their will on the country and reward those who had put them there. In essence, it was the ability of the federal government to wrest the distribution of wealth from the States through the tax code.

The conduct of any legislative body is determined by a set of rules for the introduction, debate and passage of new laws. With the limits of Congress' power now expanded they only required the implementation of rules that would cement that power. They proceeded to install rules of procedure that gave them control of committees through which all legislation must pass and the leader of the ruling party the power to stop the legislative process on any bill not to the party's liking. When a party gained control of the Congress and the Presidency it could do just about anything it wished. Fortunately, this has happened on only a few occasions and even when it has, some members of the party, along with the opposition were able to stem an otherwise total assault on the prohibitions built into the Constitution. In the end, there are few left.

It took a while for this to evolve, the first Congress being the initiator of the very first pieces of legislation envisioned necessary and proper by the framers of its outline. It was never intended to be a government but the operation and administration of a mutual defense pact and the standardization of elements of the country's economy in order for it to be uniform among the States. Its power was limited to the defense and general welfare of the United States. Its only power over individuals were those relating to persons who committed crimes against the nation such as counterfeiting, piracy on the high seas and treason.

The following is a list of the first actions taken by the first Congress in its session from 1789-1791:

- June 1, 1789:, Sess. 1, ch. 1, 1 Stat. 23
- July 4, 1789: Hamilton Tariff, Sess. 1, ch. 2, 1 Stat. 24
- August 7, 1789: *An Act for the establishment and support of Lighthouses, Beacons, Buoys, and Public Piers*, Sess. 1, ch. 9, 1 Stat. 53
- September 2, 1789: Treasury Act[1]
- September 24, 1789: Judiciary Act of 1789, Sess. 1, ch. 20, 1 Stat. 73
- March 1, 1790: Census of 1790, Sess. 2, ch. 2, 1 Stat. 101
- March 26, 1790: Naturalization Act of 1790, Sess. 2, ch. 3, 1 Stat. 103
- April 10, 1790: Patent Act, Sess. 2, ch. 7, 1 Stat. 109
- May 26, 1790: Southwest Ordinance, Sess. 2, ch. 14, 1 Stat. 123
- May 31, 1790: Copyright Act of 1790, Sess. 2, ch. 15, 1 Stat. 124
- July 6, 1790: Residence Act, Sess. 2, ch. 28, 1 Stat. 130
- July 22, 1790: Indian Intercourse Act of 1790, Sess. 2, ch. 33, 1 Stat. 137
- August 4, 1790: Funding Act of 1790, Sess. 2, ch. 34, 1 Stat. 138
- February 25, 1791: First Bank of the United States, Sess. 3, ch. 10, 1 Stat. 191

- March 3, 1791: <u>Whiskey Act</u>, Sess. 3, ch. 15, 1 <u>Stat. 199</u>

It is clear from the list that it conformed pretty well to the restrictions imposed on the powers of Congress and were for the most part merely administrative necessities. The exceptions were the precursors of the rift that was soon to develop when the Congress overstepped its authority. The rift eventually led to the Civil War and the schism between the major political parties that has usurped the power of the people and invested it with the federal government.

The first was the Hamilton Tariff that was passed in conjunction with Congress' power to raise money through tariffs. The tariffs were set on goods surplus to the States. Although uniform throughout the United States it heavily favored the North and its mercantile interests in providing it protection for its own manufactures. It did not help the South and since most of the South's exports and the North's imports came from Britain, it was feared its imposition would strain already cool relations between the former combatants.

One might argue that imposing a tariff on surplus goods was technically a bill of attainder that is prohibited not only by the federal Constitution but that of most States. A bill of attainder is an imposition by government on an individual or group. It originated in England and was one of the provisions of the Magna Carta, the document that wrested control of much of government from the King of England in his power to tax. The Knights, or Lords who were given land for their fealty feared, and rightly so, that if the King could tax or otherwise punish them individually, he could in essence ruin them and replace them with others who would certainly pledge their fealty in exchange for land.

The tax benefited the North more so than the South as it was a means to protect their fledgling industries. The South could not mount much of a challenge or justify an argument on this basis.

This was left to another piece of legislation, the Whiskey Act.

The Whiskey Act targeted a specific industry for taxation, those domestic producers who manufactured alcohol. The objection to it by those it impacted most resulted in a revolt in Pennsylvania by producers who refused to pay the tax. The tax affected mostly those on the western frontier along the Appalachian Mountains where whiskey was often the currency paid for work. It therefore hit the poor the hardest. The resultant conflict was called the Whiskey Rebellion and eventually resulted in the use of federal troops to quell it. Alcohol would be the cause of a revolt of a different type in the 1920s and is a very good illustration of why the framers specifically prohibited legislation such as bills of attainder that have been the cornerstone of the disparity of the tax laws passed ever since.

The Patent Act, though perfectly constitutional, is essentially the protection of monopoly. It and the later copy-write laws enable the holders a monopoly for a particular period. It again is a carryover from British Law designed to protect and reward intellectual property. The consequences however, deny competition to form and drive down the monopoly price and hence its practicality can be seriously questioned as it denies the consumer the lowest price. Copyright protection may be another thing in that it would seem feasible to prevent profit on plagiarism. In reality, neither is easily enforceable, particularly outside the country and should never have been treated as a subject matter for a Constitution. Its inclusion as full provision that states Congressional encouragement has since morphed into a funding source for researchers and all forms of the arts. It has become so insidious that firms have been established whose whole effort is the production of grant applications.

The biggest culprit of course is the act that established the first national bank. I claim it was a legal means to enable the biggest extortion of the American Public and describe it detail in chapter 16. It was power given to a separate private corporation to collect taxes to retire the debt incurred by the Continental Congress and the States, to fund the national government and to establish a common currency. Its successor was the Treasury Department as we know it today. It was an act that would be repeated with the creation of the Federal Reserve system that put private banks in full control of the monetary system and its distribution through the already unconstitutional tax system.

Chapter 18
Immigration and Naturalization

Article 1 Section 9 of the United States Constitution reads; 'The migration or importation of such persons as any of the States now existing shall think proper to admit, shall not be prohibited by the Congress prior to the year one thousand eight hundred and eight, but a tax or duty may be imposed on such importation, not exceeding ten dollars for each person.

The privilege of the writ of habeas corpus shall not be suspended, unless when in cases if rebellion or invasion the public safety may require it.

No bill of attainder or ex post facto law shall be passed. No capitation or other direct, tax shall be laid unless in proportion to the census or enumeration herein before directed to be taken.

No capitation, or other direct, tax shall be laid, unless in proportion to the census or enumeration herein before directed to be taken.

No tax or duty shall be laid on articles exported rom any State.

No preference shall be given by a regulation of commerce or revenue to the ports of one State over those of another; nor shall vessels bound to, or from, one State, be obliged to enter, clear, or pay duties in another.

No money shall be drawn from the treasury, but in consequence of appropriations made by law; and a regular statement of account of the receipts and expenditures of public money shall be published from time to time. (italics added)

No title of nobility shall be granted by the United States; and no person holding any office of profit or trust under them, shall, without the consent of the Congress, accept of any present, emolument, office, or title of any kind whatever from any King, Prince, or foreign State."

The first paragraph has been addressed in a previous chapter but, it is well to note that the framers took the opportunity to use its application to exact a tax, one that could not be objected to by the States as the emigrates were not yet citizens of any State and therefore not otherwise taxed.

The compromise that led to counting three fifths of the slaves for the purpose of representation may have equated the slave and non-slave holding States as far as population was concerned but, it still would not suffice in distributing the tax burden. This problem, like many other since, was kicked down the road and the catchall of the Congress' ability to collect taxes, duties, imposts and excises was left in limbo for future debate.

The writ of habeas corpus is a right belonging to each citizen against illegal seizure. In the case of the Constitution as written it would only apply to those suspected of breaking federal law. That law, as far as individuals were concerned only applied to counterfeiters, pirates and those who committed treason against the United States.

A bill of attainder is a law directed at an individual or group of individuals. It originated with the Magna Carta. It was an agreement between the King and his Lords where the Lords exacted the ability to make laws for their lands. It is in essence the constitution of England. To protect themselves, the Magna Carta prevented the King from singling any of them out in response to any wrong the King may believe they committed, in particular the non-payment of levies on their estates taken as disloyalty.

As a consequence of the Magna Carta England evolved into a

Parliamentary Democracy with shared power between the Lords and representatives of the people, the Lower House. The lower, House of Commons, has since wrested effective opposition to its actions by the House of Lords. It was a transition that has since been duplicated in the United States with the selection of Senators no longer determined by the States but by its citizens. The unfortunate difference is that the Senate still has the power, it continues to use, to block legislation, namely that involving taxes, if its majority is of a different political persuasion than that of the House of Representatives. As has been alluded to elsewhere, because of the decision in McCulloch vs. Maryland that effectively removed the limits on congressional action, when the House of Representatives, the Senate and the Presidency are all in the hands of one party, there is virtually no limit on the amount of mischief they can cause.

Capitation means a head tax. Some of the States derived a portion of revenue from the poll tax, in particular those of the North or mercantile States. A capitation tax would put a burden on the slave states because the slaves had no income and therefore the burden would fall on their owners. Invoicing the States on the basis of population, the only criteria that could be easily established through the census would therefore place a heavier burden on the freemen of the slave states than on their northern brethren.

In an attempt to accommodate the effects of an economic system based on the ownership of nature's assets, the Congress, put there by the owners of these assets, has for decades tried to balance the economy to insure the bulk of these assets remain with their owners. In doing so it has allowed banker's and money holders to collect usury. In other words, steal from the unsuspecting. In the 1930s, the administration of Franklin Roosevelt attempted to rectify the imbalance then surfacing due to the plunging value of the dollar, added organized labor to the bevy of thieves already preying on the unsuspecting and the naive. The latter practice was protected for a while by tariffs on foreign imports.

When the rest of the world, primarily China, were able to prey on the cake and eat it too society by offering the same products at lower prices, the lid was off and the unemployment of now millions was lost. If it weren't for the buy American position of the government on the military industrial sector of our economy and the jobs that can only be pursued in the country, there would hardly be any production jobs at all. Only the government, stealing through the borrowing and distribution of currency through welfare keeps the entire country from erupting into chaos.

Several of the next paragraphs restrict the sources of income that the federal government can extract from the States. The final kicker comes in the paragraph italicized above. If my interpretation of first power given Congress was a requirement for an annual balanced budget this paragraph should remove all doubt. "No money shall be drawn from the treasury, but in consequence of appropriations made by law". The language speaks for itself and explanation is not necessary.

The ultimate paragraph appears to prevent the pedaling of influence by officials of government. You will note however that it does not exempt individuals wishing to obtain favors. The reason is that it is money that put those individuals in place to be able to profit from the practice and they must continue to employ their position in favor of those who put them there or be replaced. Term limits will not solve the problem only spread the wealth more liberally. It will only stop when not only the recipient gets punished but the giver as well. It was however a practice in the States and in the government of England from whence they all came. Bad habits are hard to break, particularly when they are beneficial.

Chapter 19
Prohibitions to the States

Article 1 Section 10 of the Constitution sets out the limits that State governments have agreed to abide by as a consequence of their mutual agreement to join together for their mutual defense and welfare. It is reproduced in its entirety below:

"No State shall enter into any treaty, alliance, or confederation; grant letters of marque and reprisal; coin money; emit bills of credit; make anything but gold and silver coin a tender in payment of debts; pass any bill of attainder, ex post facto law, or law impairing the obligation of contracts, or grant any title of nobility.

No State shall, without the consent of the Congress, lay any imposts or duties on imports or exports, except what may be absolutely necessary for executing its inspection laws; and the net produce of all duties and imposts, laid by any state on imports or exports, shall be for the use of the treasury of the United States.

No State shall, without the consent of the Congress, lay any duty of tonnage, keep troops, or ships of war in time of peace, enter into any agreement or compact with another State, or with a foreign power, or engage in war, unless actually invaded, or in such imminent danger as will not admit of delay." It was Benjamin Franklin who, in 1789 in a letter to a friend wrote, "Our Constitution is in actual operation; everything appears to promise that it will last; but in this world, nothing is certain but death and taxes". It was another who also said "the power to tax is the power to destroy". The framers of the Constitution allowed that government could only tax for certain things and all for the defense of people's lives, liberties and property. It was for this reason, and this reason alone Congress and the legislatures of the States were given the power by the people to exact the cost of that service through taxes.

The States derived their government's income directly from their citizens mostly through poll and property taxes. It was imposed on so-called freemen, those who owned property, because they were the only ones who had the gold or silver to pay them. The States relied on these capitation taxes for their revenue, including the southern States. They did not agree to this method to fund the federal government or account for the State's representation in the Congress because the northern, or mercantile states, would get unequal representation in exchange for paying more of the tax burden. This dilemma was temporarily solved, at least as far as representation was concerned, but not the taxing issue. The federal government was required then to derive its income solely through tariffs, excises, impost and the like that could be imposed on anything other than people as individuals. At the same time, the federal government was the sole recipient of such funds and the section of the Constitution cited above clearly spells out that the States could not utilize these types of taxes to fund their governments as they had when they had to fund the protection previously provided by the English government.

The house of cards they built by this compromise could never have survived, no matter how the federal government chose to fund its operations because the natural wealth distribution was always going to be unequal and the addition of new States altered that inequality in favor of the mercantilists who being in favor of big government would ultimately take complete control. If you doubt this, I ask you to examine the policies of both the Republican and Democrat parties and you will confirm that the only difference between the two is how fast they want the country to evolve into a party dictatorship.

The house of cards did not take long to begin tottering when in the very first Congress Alexander Hamilton, the treasury secretary succeeded in getting President Washington to sign into law the National Bank Act, thereby grabbing hold of the nation's purse strings, in essence controlling its economy through taxation. The act was clearly beyond the powers yielded to the Congress but was never challenged. Thomas Jefferson the secretary of state and Edmond Randolph the attorney general obviously thought so because they both advised Washington against signing it. Jefferson and even James Madison thought this issue unresolved and prepared resolutions (Virginia and Kentucky Resolutions 1798-1799) passed by both State legislatures citing a States right to challenge the authority of the federal government. The mercantile north, then in control of the Congress, did not agree and the challenge was never brought to the Supreme Court. The argument was raised over the passage of the Alien and Sedition Act but the passage of the National Bank Act was not lost on the memory of those who drafted these resolutions.

A system whereby a law may be passed and enforced and then found unconstitutional cannot last. It is a system destined to dictatorship, whether by an individual or group representing 51%. The clear example is the recent passage of the Affordable Care Act (Obamacare). When challenged by the States, the law had been passed and was being implemented while the suit brought by the States was delayed and detoured by the Executive Branch until the Supreme Court was able to find a way to justify the law that was unconstitutional on its face. The Congress has no power to require individuals to buy anything, let alone pay for someone else because they cannot afford it. Mandating people pay to educate someone else's children is another example.

The very first revenue generator was a tax on imports. The amount charged varied by commodity and was therefore a bill of attainder, prohibited by the Constitution because it singled out certain goods for lower tariffs in order to placate the domestic producers of equal or similar goods. Every tax law passed since has the same character, that of favoring one group or domestic producers or a segment of the population given the exception of non-payment.

State constitutions, like that of the federal government are compacts between the freeholders of the State and its elected government for the sole purpose of the protection of their lives, their liberties and their property. Like the feudal background from which they came, the American colonists divided their territory into counties and then into towns in order to provide government, or better, their enforcing power through its police as close to the people as possible. The reason, no longer applicable, was distance and time of response. Like the States are to a federal entity, the counties are to the State, wherein the State has jurisdiction over those living outside a county on State land, the State's only constituency are the counties themselves and those living in unincorporated territories and for the sole purpose of protecting them from foreign encroachment and residence of the State from outside the unincorporated land. In Maine, there is no land outside of the jurisdiction of delineated counties except for that owned by the federal government. It is why crimes committed on federal land such as the robbery of a U. S. Post Office is a federal and not a state crime. Also, the robbery of a bank is a state crime that the federal government has made a federal crime although it takes place on privately-owned premises.

These laws and kidnapping, the selling and transportation of drugs and other crimes that can conceivably be committed in one state by a person fleeing to another, the federal government has usurped and actually thwarted the ability of state law enforcement to enforce the law outside their jurisdictions. It merely requires the mutual cooperation that implies you catch my criminals and I'll catch yours. The ultimate in this move is already underway with federal FBI operations in every State and major metropolitan area. I agree that law enforcement is necessary but I hasten to add that if the punishment proscribed by God in the law as given to Moses and adopted by Christians and Muslims alike were applied there would perhaps be far less crime. That punishment, for murders and thieves was stoning to death. You need not believe me, just read the book of Deuteronomy.

The most significant of these prohibitions was the making of gold and silver as the only means for the payment of debts. It was the death knell of the barter economy and the crowning achievement of the mercantile faction (Federalists). It cemented their control over the economy as had been the case with every government previously conceived regardless of type.

Chapter 20
The Judiciary and the Courts

Article III of the U. S. Constitution assigned the judicial power of the United States to a Supreme Court and such inferior courts as the Congress shall establish. That power "shall extend to all cases in law and equity arising out of this Constitution, the laws of the United States and treaties made or which shall be made under their authority; to all cases affecting ambassadors other public ministers or consuls; to all cases of admiralty and maritime jurisdiction; to controversies between two or more States; between a State and citizens of another State; between citizens of different States; between citizens of the same State claiming lands under grants of different States and between a State, or the citizens thereof and foreign States citizens or subjects".

The concessions made by the Federalists (mercantilists)) in obtaining the agreement of the anti-Federalists. contained the seeds that would eventually undo the concessions and pave the way to changing the form of government envisioned by the latter from a republic to a democracy, the form that some of them feared. The establishment of a national bank in the first Congress would give the Federalists control of the economy. It only left controlling the law to complete the coup and they also accomplished this in the first Congress with the passage of the Judiciary Act in September of 1789.

The key provision of this act is contained in Section 25 and is cited in part below:

"And it be it further enacted, that a final judgment of decree in any suit, in the highest court of law or equity of a State, in which a decision in the suit could be had, where is drawn in question the validity of a treaty or state of, or an authority exercised under the United States and the decision is against their validity; or where is drawn in question the construction of any clause of the Constitution, or of a treaty, or statute of, or an authority exercised under any State, on the ground their being repugnant to the Constitution, treaties or laws of the United States and the decision is in favor of such their validity, or where is drawn in question the construction of any clause of the Constitution, or of a treaty, or statue of, or commission held under the States and the decision is against the title, right, privilege, or exemption specially set up or claimed by either party, under such clause of the said Constitution treaty, statute, or commission, may be re-examined and reversed or affirmed in the Supreme Court of the United States upon a writ of error, the citation being signed by the chief justice, or judge or chancellor of the court rendering or passing the judgement or decree complained of, or by a justice of the Supreme Court of the United States, in the same manner and under the same regulations and the writ shall have the same effect, as if the judgment or decree complained of had been rendered or passed in a circuit court and the proceedings upon the reversal shall also be the same, except that the Supreme Court, instead of remanding the cause for a final decision as before provided, may, at their discretion, if the cause shall have been once remanded before, proceed to a final decision of the same, and award execution." If this is not the longest sentence ever written it ranks right on up there.

On its passage, it had the effect of making the Supreme Court the arbiter of Constitutionality, taking the final authority away from the Congress by their override of a Presidential veto and that of the President as the first line of defense while at the same time politicizing the court itself. The Federalists, gaining control of the Congress, the Presidency and the Courts could pass whatever law they pleased and it would stand Constitutional muster. It caused the widening of the rift between the Federalists and the anti-Federalists that eventual led to the Civil War. It is exactly what the Democrats did in the 1930s that has created the rift between Democrats and Republicans uncharacteristically called the have-nots and the haves.

The Constitution precluded the States from using the Supreme Court to question the actions of the Congress. You will note in reading the Article that controversies between the States and the Federal Government were not covered in the charter of the Court's authority. The purpose of the omission was to throttle the ability of any State or a group of them from questioning the acts of the Congress or those in which the Congress and the Executive could collude to pass. The remainder of this massive law set the stage for the federal government to usurp and assume powers even the States themselves did not have

The existence of a separate federal judiciary had been controversial during the debates over the ratification of the Constitution. Anti-Federalists had denounced the judicial power as a potential instrument of national tyranny. Indeed, of the ten amendments that eventually became the Bill of Rights five (the fourth through the eighth) dealt primarily with judicial proceedings. Even after ratification, some opponents of a strong judiciary urged that the federal court system be limited to a Supreme Court and perhaps local admiralty judges. The Congress, however, decided to establish a system of federal trial courts with broader jurisdiction, thereby creating an arm for enforcement of national laws within each state. The power of the Supreme Court was again confirmed in the case of McCulloch vs. Maryland (17 US 316) by Chief Justice John Marshall.

It is reasonable for the Supreme Court to have jurisdiction in disputes between States but not a dispute between individuals of different States or between a State and a citizen of another State.

Instead, the Constitution need have only modified the language of Article IV Section 1 that should have read:

"Full faith and credit shall be given in each State to the public acts and judgments enacted and arrived at in every other State. Upon application, by any State, the federal authority is empowered to assist the State in the apprehension of criminals and the satisfaction of judgements and the States shall cooperate in that effort. Failure to do so shall be considered an offense against the United States and punishable by fine or imprisonment or both of a States chief enforcement executive."

Such a clause is in keeping with the power to regulate commerce between the States but it prevents the federal government from directly involving itself in a State's regulation of businesses in their State irrespective of whether the business is engaged in interstate or intrastate business. Disputes between individuals or corporations of one state and individuals or corporations of another should be settled in the State of the aggrieved party. The federal government may however establish standards to insure punishment of criminals or violators of regulations are equitably applied to the citizens of one own State and citizens of another. This implies a requirement to render suspected criminals to the jurisdiction where their crime was alleged to be committed. In other words, there should be no safe haven, which is not now the case when a State can refuse to extradite a criminal charged with murder because it has abolished the death penalty and the State to which the criminal is to be remanded has not.

It would have enable the creation of the Federal Bureau of Investigation (FBI) and the U. S. Marshalls service to provide assistance to States in the apprehension of criminals and the enforcement of legal judgments when two or more States were involved. The only federal laws involving criminal offenses would be the crimes of counterfeiting, piracy, treason against the country and those committed on the high seas. The only commercial judgments that would involve the federal judiciary would be those commercial acts by States of citizens of a State and a foreign entity or government where a treaty existed honoring the laws of each as indicated above between the individual States.

We are reminded that according to God's law as rendered to Moses, the punishment for criminal offenses set out in the Ten Commandments was stoning to death. It was meant both to be a deterrent and if that was insufficient to purge the society of law breakers. There were no jails and the punishment of acts considered abhorrent but not criminal were punished by banishment. One such named was homosexuality. It is unfortunate however, that the economic system we have adopted requires one to work in order to survive, meaning if you cannot work you must rely on others to share their surplus or steal it from them, thereby demanding you undertake criminal acts. Government has stepped in and become the charitable giver through the tax system in order to dissuade people from becoming thieves, a pursuit that has obvious limits and is doomed to failure.

The era of big government had started and its conquest of a Republic was complete before it even had a chance to begin. Since 1789 we have morphed not even into a democracy but a form of fascism wherein the means of production are in private ownership but heavily regulated by a government that caters to the desires of minority groups in order to maintain power. It is a method of governance that has a form but no single identifier because the political parties that espouse it are themselves split between their definition of what constitutes big or bigger central governance.

Chapter 21
State Sovereignty and Reciprocity

Article IV of the United States Constitution reaffirms the sovereignty of the States and the rules for admission of new States. Section 1 requires that each State honor the laws and acts of another, Section 2 requires that accused criminals from one State shall at the request of their Governor be returned to the State in which the alleged crime was committed. It also requires that persons held to service or labor in one State shall not be discharged from such service or labor, but shall be delivered up on claim of the party to whom such service or labor may be due.

This latter part referred not only to slaves, but indentured servants. The latter being debtors who were bound to service of the one holding the debt. In England when you owed someone money and could not pay you could, at the debt holders option, perform service to work off the debt or go to debtor's prison. If, slaves were considered property as they were by the southerners who owned them or persons, as northerners considered them this provision applies in that both property and persons must be remanded to their owner or debt holder if requested by the State from which they fled or were taken.

The Fugitive Slave Act of 1850 was a fillip to the southern states and totally unnecessary since the requirement to return slaves to their owners was already the law of the land. The northern States to where many slaves had escaped became havens and the States to which they fled had no intention to return them. Many States refused to obey the law and Wisconsin's Supreme Court actually declared it unconstitutional. It further inflamed the

South's contention they were getting the short end of the stick from the Federalist dominated government not only by way of taxes, but by being above the law. The accumulation of the abuses led to the Civil War.

The second paragraph of Section 3 gives the Congress the power "to make all needful rules and regulations respecting the territory or other property belonging to the United States and nothing in the Constitution shall be so construed as to prejudice claims of the United States, or of any particular State". The Treaty of Paris that ended the Revolutionary War ceded all lands owned by the King not sold to private individuals and groups. The subsequent Louisiana Purchase and the ceding of Florida by Spain, and western territories ceded by Mexico that included the future States of California, Arizona and New Mexico, made the federal government the world's largest land owner. When additional States were admitted to the union all the land within their assigned boundaries was not ceded to the States but retained by the federal government. The exception was Texas that had freed itself from Mexico and was a separate Republic and California. Texas requested to join the Union as a protective act. Canada was offered statehood but declined.

Texas retained ownership of the land within its borders that had not been sold to resident Texans. California on the other hand was replete with old Spanish land grants as had the original 13 American Colonies and disputes over actual ownership went on for decades. The long and the short was it provided a virtual treasure trove for federal politicians to be first in line to buy and then resell government owned land. It was a method used by the King of Saudi Arabia who awarded large tracts of land as rewards to the Princes who in turn sold them to get the cash. This went on for several years until the bulk of it was sold.

The law, at the same time voided any claims by the States that had received vaguely specified grants by the King, in particular

Virginia who had original claims extending to the Mississippi River. When the land was all gone the politicians had to resort to direct access to the treasury in order to make their fortunes and they have succeeded well in doing just that, all attempts to quell or even temper it notwithstanding.

Chapter 22
Amending the Constitution

Article V of the United States Constitution is that part of the compromise that became the Constitution that would allow it to be amended in the event it became necessary. It would take two thirds of both houses of Congress to propose them or a convention of two thirds of the States and then ratified by three fourths of the States. The exception was that "no amendment made prior to 1808 shall in any manner affect the first and fourth clauses in the ninth section of the first article; and that no state, without its consent, shall be deprived of its equal suffrage in the Senate". The referenced clauses were those that permitted the importation of slaves until 1808 and how they impacted a State's representation in the Congress.

Both the Federalists and the anti-Federalists (State's righters) were content with the bargains struck at the Constitutional Convention. It is why it was offered to individual State legislatures on a take- it or leave-it basis and when approved by 9 of the 13 States would be difficult, if not impossible to change. Underlying the entire agreement was an understanding that a so-called Bill-of Rights, which few could agree on was left for future deliberation. More on this in another chapter.

It has been said that the framers acknowledged the Constitution was not perfect and therefore provided the means to correct its imperfections. If this is true they should have made it easier to correct mistakes when they surfaced. On the contrary, those who got the better of the bargain wanted to insure that correcting what gave them the edge would be difficult to erase.

Little did the States realize that in agreeing to the power of the federal government to "coin money and regulate the value thereof" and the State's prohibition against, making "anything but gold and silver coin a tender in payment of debts" provided fodder for the mercantile (Federalist) States to at first disadvantage the slave States and will ultimately bring about the end of the government itself in due course.

It was Adam Smith who explained the value of money as a means of exchange and attempted to explain the inefficiencies of barter, or exchange of goods. His explanations were unfortunately predicated on the use of gold and silver then the universally accepted means of exchange. It was a satisfactory assumption when gold and silver were being added to the economy with regularity but, so were an increasing number of participants. Stabilize the number of participants while continuing to produce more gold and silver and their weakness as a measure of exchange becomes readily apparent. They are not consumed in trade but accumulate thereby increasing their price as soon as its cost to produce exceeded its imputed value as exchange.

Barter on the other hand is demeaned as inefficient because it relies on a double coincidence of wants or, both parties need to have what the other wants. The continuing division of labor due to the growing numbers of participants exacerbates the situation because more and more people become removed from the direct access to the most basic exchange, food. Barter is sharing. When there was no currency the braves hunted, the women, children and elderly grew the crops and made everything they needed. As the tribe grew families specialized because hunting and farming no longer required additional labor to expand production, simply work more efficiently. One family produced the clothes, another did the hunting, another the farming and they all pitched in to build the tepees. Further growth in numbers found some unwilling to bear the burden of work and still got a share and the system broke down. The Plymouth Colony is a classic example. Additional labor-saving devices, coupled with an increase in numbers resulted in more hours available but no work on which to occupy them. Those having those hours still had to eat.

There are three ways to survive in this world; you can earn it, you can share with those who have a surplus and are willing, or you can steal it. Benevolent governments steal from those who have a surplus through taxes and provide it to those who cannot work. When the government fears adding to the tax burden will result in its demise they resort to printing more money thereby accelerating the rate of inflation. It is a system that cannot reverse its ultimate demise unless it changes the distribution. Governments cannot and will not do this because those getting the most see to it that the ones they help elect or rule are duly rewarded for not changing the system.

The contract (Constitution) between the States created a third party, the federal government, that was to protect them from foreign invasion, break down the trade barriers between them, prevent them from recurring and to standardize their economies around a single currency. The Federalists made it look like the anti-Federalists had gotten the best of the bargain when it appeared they would shoulder the bulk of the cost on a State by State basis, even giving the antifederalists more representation than they would get if only the non-slave population were counted. The euphoria must have been short lived because when the Congress convened for the first time the acts that were passed showed that the Federalists had the edge and were the first to cut into the limitations on the powers of the Congress, the jurisdiction of the federal courts and the passage of prohibited "bills of attainder" with the first tariff measure. The downhill slide had begun. Along the way, the State governments became for all purposes redundant.

Chapter 23
The Bill of Rights

The inclusion of a bill of rights was a controversial issue in the Constitutional Convention. Most of the States had already incorporated such provisions in their state constitutions. Many in the convention claimed that inclusion in the Constitution was unnecessary since the federal government was not sovereign and was merely a compact between sovereign States for their mutual protection and limited power over the actions of the sovereign States and certainly not over the people of the States with the exceptions of counterfeiters, pirates and those who committed treason against the United States. Some claimed that such an inclusion could not be all inclusive of the rights held by the States and the people. It was a concern that Madison thought he addressed with the tenth amendment. However, as promised the State conventions in order to secure their adoption of the Constitution, ten of the twelve proposed amendments were ratified in December of 1791.

As a mutual defense pact, the States saw safety in numbers. It is why they agreed to the compact when it appeared they would be at the mercy of the country they denounced and fought a war to free themselves of it. It was also fear of others such as Spain and France who might covet more land than they already had in the New World. In agreeing, they pledged their militias and renounced the right to war on each other and to submit to a single currency and free trade between them. It is what the citizens of each State agreed to in their own constitutions for themselves. The only citizens the federal government had jurisdiction over where those who were common enemies of the States as a whole;

counterfeiters, pirates and those who committed treason against the country.

Even the States could not, under their constitutions, make any but reasonable laws and regulations for the defense and welfare of all their citizens. That is protection of their lives, liberties and property. It is the police power, while at the same time the citizens could, in the absence of the police, defend themselves. If they were killed, their liberties infringed or their property stolen, the police power gave the State the ability to hunt down and punish the miscreants whereas individually they were virtually powerless to do so. Those that did were called vigilantes but not all could afford to be so they mutually agreed to pay for the State to fill that role.

The dangers in any contract and the Constitution is basically a contract between the States and a federal government of their creation is that one party wants to add scope without payment and the other wants to provide less than the other thought he paid for. I once had an auditor tell me he thought a contractor shouldn't be able to charge more for extra work if he didn't have to provide any extra manpower for its execution. It is difficult to reason with that type of mindset. Getting the States to pay for the service provided was not a problem because the Congress was given the power to "tax for the defense and welfare of the United States". The problem was their having to be taxed for services for which they did not contract. It is the latter that has gotten us into trouble.

On the defense side alone are costs that no rational individual can justify as being solely for the defense of the country. No country would consider declaring war on the United States because the cost in human life, theirs, would be so high as to not justify the effort. Like Switzerland in World War II, Hitler knew the cost in German lives if he dared invade Switzerland. He knew the same would be true if he invaded England. His only resource was to keep it weak enough so that it would not come to the aid of those he chose to conquer.

The issue remains as to how to limit the government to perform only those services for which you contracted and were willing to pay for? The Bill of Rights prohibiting the federal government from taking certain actions against individuals couldn't insure it, because in writing them it indirectly admitted the federal government could actually enact and enforce the actions they were now being prohibited from doing. They became the crack that John Marshall exploited in his Supreme Court ruling that allowed the Congress broad interpretation of its powers within a framework of those not prohibited.

Madison has said, "if all men were angels there would be no need of government". The anti- Federalists, trying to protect themselves from a possible expansion of government wanted, in addition to the limitations imposed on the Congress by Article 1 Sections 8 and 9, championed the inclusion of a Bill of Rights. The Federalists, having already insured they could pretty much do as the pleased if they held the Congress and the Presidency put up little fight against its inclusion. Ten of those proposed were considered sufficient to protect the rights of the people and survived the debates. The Federalists succeeded in eliminating the two that might cause them difficulty, the first being the means of determining the number of representatives in the House. The second was a clear statement of the separation of powers between the various branches of government.

Had the initial method of determining the number of representatives been left as originally determined, one representative for every 50,000, the House would now consist of over 6,000 members. The Congress has capped the number by law to 435 with no state having less than one Representative with the remainder reapportioned based on population. The consequence is that when a new census shows a shift in population and one State grows in population faster than another it obtains a larger portion of the representation. Unlike the British Parliament where the districts are fixed, as well as the number of parliamentary seats, the U. S. House of Representatives leaves the method of districting to the States. The consequence is the political parties Gerrymander the district boundaries in an attempt to insure the reelection of winners when they have the power to do so.

One of the proposed amendments was, "the powers delegated by the Constitution to the government of the United States, shall be exercised as therein appropriated, so that the Legislative shall never exercise the powers vested in the Executive or Judicial; nor the Executive the powers vested in the Legislative or Judicial; nor the Judicial the powers vested in the Legislative or Executive." This is but an affirmation of what the anti-federalists believed they had already built into the original agreement. It however still left open the consequences of non- compliance which is the weakness of any law or regulation.

The Executive branch of government has been making law from the very beginning in that the broad mandate given the Congress is ineffectual until the laws resulting from the power to make them require detailed elaboration to make them effective. Most Congressmen haven't the wherewithal to draft but a broad outline of legislation, leaving the Executive or enforcement branch to fill in the blanks so to speak such that the final law will pass muster as regards to the limitations of action imposed by Article 1 Sections 8 and 9. That is they are safe from challenge by the parties on which they are imposed. The Affordable Care Act, drafted by the Obama Administration exceeded 2400 pages and probably took two or more years to draft. That it never saw the light of day in the Congress until its time for passage and that few, if any had read but a summary developed by their staffs is illustrated by the comment of the then Speaker of the House, Nancy Pelosi, "we have to pass it before we know what's in it".

That the system has been corrupted is readily evident is the case of the Affordable Care Act or Obamacare. Making health insurance affordable is a noble objective but it was never a cause to be championed by the federal government as originally conceived. Even the proponents of the act, that passed it on a pure partisan vote and was approved by the President who championed it and whose administration actually wrote the legislation ignored that fact. It was immediately challenged by several of the States and the general population because it was essentially a bill of attainder targeted to subsidize those who could not ordinarily afford it. The challenge, instead of taking precedence in the Supreme Court as required by Article III, the executive branch forced the challenge to the lower courts where it would languish and perhaps go away. An attempt at obtaining an injunction to stop its implementation until its constitutionality could be tested was rebuffed by the courts, ostensibly along partisan lines but believing the Congress and the President would not do anything they were unauthorized to do.

We all know how it turned out when Chief Justice Roberts and a majority of the Court upheld the law, not as the administration had envisioned it, but as a tax, which the Congress had the power to levy and the President to approve. Needless to say, they ignored the fact that the original charter gave the power to tax to the Congress but only for a limited objective of defending the States. Providing charity to a small segment of the population violates both the intent of the Constitution and its prohibition against bills of attainder. That this has now been irretrievably lost is confirmed in the first paragraph of Justice Thomas' dissent where he confirms the Congress had the power to pass such legislation but it was improperly drafted.

The assault on the Bill of Rights was not long in coming and began with the passage of the Alien and Sedition Acts. These were acts passed by the Federalists in 1798 and signed into law by

Federalist President John Adams. The first three dealt with immigrants and extended the time to become a citizen, allowed the deportation of certain aliens and aliens from countries hostile to the United States. The fourth dealt with persons who made false statements against the federal government. Three were repealed when Thomas Jefferson and the anti- federalists came to power. The fourth, the Alien Enemies Act, has been amended and remains in force and was last utilized by Franklin Roosevelt to inter Japanese during World War II. It was an action that spurred the writing of the Kentucky and Virginia Resolutions penned separately by Madison and Jefferson and passed by their respective legislatures which opined the States had the power to ignore federal laws they deemed unconstitutional. The Federalist States failed to agree. It was the first of many strikes at States rights that ultimately culminated in secession and the Civil War.

The assault continues against these "rights", the major battles being fought over the right to bear arms, freedom of speech and unreasonable searches and seizures. The government has not prohibited people from having firearms to protect themselves but has put so many barriers in the way to obtaining them that only criminals can still obtain them cheaply or steal them from others.

The Homeland Security Administration is in the process of searching, X-raying or otherwise examining all passengers at airports on the pretext they may be carrying illicit materials that could bring down an airliner. One could consider such invasion of one's person definitely without probable cause unreasonable but such is not the case as the public has accepted the practice as in their best interest and have raised no objections. On the other hand, a person stopped for a law violation is immune from a search of his person or his vehicle or his home as unreasonable and if narcotics or illegal weapons are found it is deemed an unreasonable act by the police and the law breaker cannot be charged. A police state is created when government fears its citizens will accumulate arms and are in collusion to overthrow the government. Our government is so insecure that it is ready to make sure no actual criminal gets punished so long as the people who are being subjugated by the burden of law are made powerless to topple it.

The last two, amendments IX and X were a vain attempt to limit the powers of the federal government and maximize the rights of citizens. Neither of these objectives can be achieved when the Congress, the Executive and the Judiciary are of a single mind as has occurred on several occasions one such in particular, that of the administration of Franklin Roosevelt where unconstitutional legislation that had a profound impact on the economy breezed through all three branches unscathed.

Chapter 24
Limitation of the Federal Courts

The eleventh amendment to the U. S. Constitution had its origins in the act of Congress that established the federal judiciary. It came to a head in the case of Chisholm v. Georgia (2 US 419) where a federal court denied State sovereignty and awarded a judgement to the plaintiff Chisolm against the State of Georgia. Plaintiff argued the State had surrendered its sovereignty when it signed the U. S. Constitution. The case was argued before the Supreme Court by the United States Attorney General Edmond Randolph. The State of Georgia declined to appear. It caused such a furor among the anti-Federalists that they mounted a successful campaign and got the amendment passed that clarified the judicial powers of the federal government.

Under Article III Section 2 of the U. S. Constitution the federal judiciary was given the power over civil matters between the citizens of different States and the citizens of a State against their own government. A sovereign State, by definition, could not be sued unless it agreed. The case removed this protection but it was restored and reaffirmed by the amendment. The federal government is not sovereign but its actions and officers are provided immunity by the very first amendment to the Constitution which gives the people the right to petition the government a redress of their grievances. Unfortunately, it does not mandate the government actually address or even respond to them. Does the saying you can't fight city hall take on new emphasis?

Chapter 25
Separating the Vote for President

The twelfth amendment to the U. S. Constitution came about when Thomas Jefferson, an anti-Federalist became vice President under the Federalist President John Adams. It was the time that the Federalists were the dominant party and to avoid this occurrence again they passed and the States ratified the amendment that separated the electoral college vote into a vote for President and another for Vice President. Heretofore the electors got two votes, one for whomever they chose and another whomever they chose so long as he was not from the same State as the elector. The consequence of the original system was always the possibility the candidate getting the second most votes and automatically becoming Vice President could be of a different political persuasion as the President. With the President's power of the veto to prevent the Congress from expanding the reach of government, the Federalists could not have such a situation. They at the time were the so-called party in power throughout the country and therefore could affect the change. They failed to believe their political fortunes would succumb to popular spirit as more States entered the Union.

George Washington, in his farewell address cautioned against political parties splitting the country. He was speaking from strength because Federalists, like himself, controlled the federal government and the majority of the States. This hegemony would not last long and the Federalist movement was usurped by the anti-Federalists with the elections of Thomas Jefferson and James Madison. The Federalists had already sowed the seeds of fracture with the laws already passed such as the Judiciary Act and the

National Bank Act that gave the federal government control of the treasury that the schism no longer revolved about federal versus States rights, but who gained the most from the tax code. The raid on the treasury had begun and the ones who had the money got to keep more by shifting the tax burden to those who had less. He who has the gold makes the rules.

The twelfth amendment did not solve the problem, if indeed there was a problem. The political parties were still able to skew the outcome through various methods because the Constitution still left the selection of electors to the legislatures of the several States. The States still vary as to how electors are chosen but nearly all now allow the political parties to nominate the candidates for elector. Some States require the electors to vote for the candidate who receives the most popular votes and some mandate that be by district. Only two, Maine and Nevada still go by popular vote in each district for the electors who represent the number of House members and the two who represent the two Senators. This enables the candidate with the less popular votes to win more of the electoral votes because of population differences.

Even when the parties get to choose the electors and its electors get to choose, not all States require these electors to vote for their parties candidate. This has happened in several elections but it had no consequence on the ultimate outcome. There very well could come a day when it can and a few sleepers could possibly throw the election into the House of Representatives. Only 30 States require electors to vote for their party's nominee and fine the "faithless" elector and replace him, negating his vote. This year one Texas Republican elector has indicated he will not cast his vote for the States Republican winner, Donald Trump. If his vote and that of others of similar mood could result in a constitutional crisis however, these votes will likely be discounted and replaced by more loyal electors.

The objective of the electoral college was to ensure that anyone elected to the Presidency be commonly known as qualified by those who were in actual position to judge or be persuaded by those who knew the candidate. A popular vote was never contemplated because of this condition being impossible on a country wide basis, even by men of means as were those who had suffrage in colonial times. In fact a popular vote was not even taken until 1824 when Andrew Jackson got the most popular votes but lost to John Quincy Adams.

Chapter 26
Slavery

The thirteenth amendment to the U. S. Constitution was an attempt to abolish slavery or involuntary servitude except as punishment for a crime. It was an attempt to abolish the practice of slavery, it being defined then as involuntary servitude. A slave is a person devoid of freedom and personal rights and is chattel to another as a consequence of war or sale. An indentured servant on the other hand undertaking involuntary servitude is a debtor to someone willing to accept service as payment of debt. The framers did not want to abolish the practice of indenture for payment of debts but wanted to abolish slavery or the consideration of persons as property to be bought and sold. In ignoring the distinction, the framers of the amendment erred by not actually abolishing slavery but defining it the same as indentured servitude. All the slave owner had to do was claim he was owed room and boards by his former slave and could then be returned to labor indefinitely because his debt would be ongoing. In order to overcome this error, they contrived the fourteenth amendment which compounded the felony by mixing it with the readmission of the States who had seceded from the Union.

The intent to free the existing slaves and abolish the practice together and consider the former slaves as citizens entitled to all the rights and privileges of citizens of the State in which they resided could have been satisfactorily accomplished by the following:

"All persons brought to or born in the United States as slaves shall, from the date of ratification of the amendment, be considered "Freemen" and enjoy all the rights and privileges afforded all of that State's "Freemen" and shall be considered a citizen of that

State and of the United States."

The timing of the amendment is important because it was accomplished when the seceded States were no longer represented in the Congress or considered part of the Union. If it had been drafted and ratified as suggested, the fourteenth amendment's first two clauses would not have been necessary and there would be no "anchor baby" problem. The citizenship of children born to foreigners who happened to be in the United States as visitors would never have become an issue.

Chapter 27
Fixing the Slavery Amendment

The fourteenth amendment is an abomination made necessary by the error in the language of the thirteenth. It construction was compounded by the fact that it had to be passed by States who had previously seceded but who were now readmitted to the Union.

Section 1 was an attempt at language suggested in chapter 26 but had to be modified to placate the now readmitted States and give them leeway in continuing to deny to their former slaves the same rights as their other citizens. It resulted first in denial of voting privileges, then separate but equal facilities and schools and the continuation of discriminatory practices against the negro race. I emphasize the negro race in order not to confuse them with the Chinese who came to California as guest workers so to speak who were not treated like property. Discriminated against at first but upon their ultimate assimilation in the population have not had to endure the legal discrimination as have those of the negro race.

Section 2 redefines the representation in the Congress of the seceding States and rescinding the compromise made to remove objections in the original document whereby slaves would count for 3/5 of a person for representation purposes and as a nonperson for tax purposes. This Section and Section 3 were another compromise to obtain the consent of the seceded States whereby they could be represented in Congress by individuals who had previously rebelled against the United States. It was just another move by the successors of the Federalist movement to enable the ultimate neutering of the States that had stalled with the Civil War.

Section 4 denied any claims by the seceding States for their expenses in waging war against the Union and obligated the seceding States to assist in paying debts incurred by the non-seceding States in pursuit of the war. Failure to accept was not an option. It was bargain sealed with a gun at their head. If they wanted protection from the United States when their creditors in Europe came to collect on their loans they had to agree. Confederate currency, like the former "Continentals" became worthless except as collectors' items and Confederate States Bonds went into default.

Chapter 28
Voting Rights

Article XV, the fifteenth amendment to the U. S. Constitution would have been totally unnecessary if the language of Article XIII had been properly written. It would have also made unnecessary legislation such as the Civil Rights Act, the Voting Rights Act all deemed necessary to legally bar the so-called evil effects of discrimination. Discrimination is a fundamental right of every human being. If you don't like broccoli no one should force you to eat it. If government can make you eat broccoli or ban you from smoking cigarettes or drinking alcohol you become nothing more than and automaton. That your discrimination really effects no one but yourself, for good or bad, is totally ignored but if 51% of you choose to engage in it and legislate it, forcing the other 49% to conform, that is democracy.

Chapter 29
The Income Tax

Article XVI the sixteenth amendment to the U. S. Constitution was made necessary by the compromise on taxation made in the original document, the growing scope of government activity due to usurpation of responsibilities that belong to the people and the economic system adopted by the making of gold and silver the only currency for the satisfaction of debts.

The scope of government constantly grew out of the expansion of powers taken by the Congress sanctioned by the Supreme Court or totally unchallenged. The majority of it took the form of bills of attainder and some through ex post facto laws, both of which are prohibited by the Constitution and by it to the States. The States were only able to cede to a federal government a share of the police power the people had surrendered to their government. The tenth amendment was written to confirm this but has been ignored as a limit to federal power.

The making of gold and silver the means of exchange would eventually inflate both silver and gold and then paper currency that was substituted for it because the actual cost of producing gold and silver finally exceed its imputed value and consequently that of the paper currency. The reason is that instead of it being consumed as spent it accumulates and each additional amount added to the supply dilutes the value of all those previously issued. The result is that costs rise and real value does not.

In 1914 the price of gold was $18 and its actual cost to produce was $18. The arbitrage that previously existed between countries where gold was mined and used as currency essentially vanished. By the 1930s the imputed value of gold had to be raised to $36 per ounce and eventually the cost to produce rose so quickly that

President Nixon finally unlinked gold and the dollar, allowing the dollar to assume a value described as the "full faith and credit of the United States". The meaning of this value has never been defined. I have however defined it in my book, "The Real Economy" as the fuel value of food that provides life and the ability to work to mine gold or anything else. The United States and several other countries still produce enough fuel in the form of kilocalories (kcal) to feed their populations and produce useful work. The book explains the direct connection, the effect on the economy of those countries who choose to ignore it, its ultimate consequences and how to change the economic system to extend human life on the planet.

Adopting a failing economic system coupled with added scope and a diminishing income dependent solely on import tariffs and other taxes the government was in need of the most logical source, the incomes of individuals. An income or direct tax was hampered by provisions of Article 1 Section 9 prohibiting a capitation or head tax unless in accordance with the enumeration prescribed in Article 1 Section 2 or the first census. As slavery had been abolished and the first census enumerated on 3/5 of the slaves, the previous conditions would result in an abomination, therefore the need for different language.

The need was great and a simple head tax could not raise enough unless it was high enough. That would unduly tax the poor who are always of the opinion the rich should pay more because they had more to protect and the result might be the loss of your seat and the downfall of the government itself. It is what happened to several successive governments in Germany after World War I, trying to pay off the war debt with printed money. Their solution was print more money that caused rampant inflation. The American solution was create a graduated system, administered by the largest bureaucracy yet created within the government, the Internal Revenue Service" but, coupled with enough loop holes that the rich could escape the full wrath of graduated system while making it appear they were actually paying more. The entire scheme has been nothing but a bill of attainder aimed at the middle class who worked for wages and salaries. It now stretches to over 70,000 pages. It generated the revenue necessary and preserved the jobs of the politicians who created it until the Great Depression.

That story is beyond the purpose set out for this series of commentaries but safe to say that despite the Great Depression and all of the downturns in the economy since, the fundamental system was flawed from the beginning, the only question of when it will come tumbling down is only a question of time.

Chapter 30
Popular Election of Senators

Amendment XVIII to the U. S. Constitution deals with the method for direct election of Senators, heretofore selected by the legislatures of each State. When the legislature is split between parties controlling each house it was difficult for the two bodies to agree on who should represent the State and in several cases States were unable to field a candidate to fill the vacancy, leaving the Senate without full representation. Washington's fears of the government becoming a political battleground were not unfounded. Because the government had expanded its charter beyond its real purpose which was the defense and welfare of the States, it had degraded to who could get more from the treasury.

Suffrage, or the right to vote during colonial times was restricted to property owners who amounted to only about 6% of the population. Over time, particularly after the Revolution, suffrage was expanded to non-property owners and in some cases even to women property owners. By the 1900's universal male suffrage became common and with the strength of the political party supposedly defending the rights of the non-property-owning class in determining who should represent them and in particular how to tax them. The early consequences of this type of selective representation resulted in the legislative bodies becoming representative of the moneyed interests and over time as suffrage expanded the bicameral legislatures becoming split along party lines. It was considered a good split in that the upper chamber could temper the rashness of the lower. Lost in this was that the government had only a limited role, that of defense of the State or the Union and that party affiliation should have made no difference. When the government however, took on the role of distributor of wealth through the tax codes interests shifted from collective to individual.

The history of the British system is interesting in that we are destined to repeat it. Our Congress is like that of the original British system where the King made law and his Lords served as advisors and administrators. This changed with the Magna Carta where the Kings power to make law was diminished and the Lords made and administered most laws. This evolved again into a Parliament where the people were represented and could make law with the consent of the Lords and the King had little if no power and was relegated to simply rubber stamping what had gotten through the Parliament. As it stands now the lower house of Parliament has created a rubber stamp of the House of Lords and the political parties are left to fight each other for control of who makes law. The battle now is over who gets to pay for the excesses of the other and the defense and welfare of the people be damned. The consequences of these excesses is a country in debt to the tune of nearly $20 trillion and growing with no possible way to pay it.

Chapter 31
Prohibition

The XVIII amendment to the Constitution prohibited the manufacture, sale or transportation of intoxicating liquors within, the importation thereof into, or the exportation thereof from the United Sates and all territories subject to the jurisdiction thereof, for beverage purposes. The Volstead Act, was passed after the amendment had been ratified by the requisite number of States.

The amendment itself was a violation of the original Constitution in that the Congress was prohibited from enacting bills of attainder that is laws not having universal application. If it were intended that the Congress could address specifics the framers of the original document would not have included this provision. In addition, the thing that was being prohibited was heretofore permitted, making the law ex post factor therefore also prohibited to the Congress.

The consequences of this violation of the law have become legion and for nearly fourteen years, until its repeal, the United States underwent the ravages of a crime spree not seen in history until the prohibition of narcotics that is still having its effects on the population and the escalation of crime.

The fact the Congress passed this act and it was sanctioned by the President and then the requisite number of States was an admission of sorts that the term welfare as used in the very first power given to Congress was not in itself a separate power and had been used as such in many preceding acts to get around the prohibitions built into the Constitution.

Chapter 32
Women's Suffrage

The nineteenth amendment to the U. S. Constitution gave women the right to vote by prohibiting States to deny them this right. The thrust to provide universal suffrage to women began in the 1800s and as new States were admitted to the Union many of them had included women among those granted suffrage. The consequences were a hodgepodge where in some States women could vote and others not. It had no impact on representation in the Congress since women were still counted in the population figures. The movement to universalize the practice gained momentum and in 1920 the amendment became law. The no taxation without representation mantra of the original colonists was now extended to the other half of the population. Not impacted were State exclusions of convicts, convicted felons and the insane or incompetent which still prevail in most states, regardless of sex.

On the surface, this action would seem appropriate but one ignores the fact that the Congress and the federal government have taken on additional scope beyond that permitted by the original Constitution's limitation. That had morphed into all forms of preferred treatment to certain groups and causes to which now would be added those peculiar to women. Now the politicians, in order to get elected or reelected had to pander to the interests of a whole new clientele and with the treasury open to all forms of chicanery they were eager to comply. The one they have been eagerly pushing is equal pay for equal work which they have successfully accomplished in the military and government employment but without much success in the private sector. The impediment there is the prohibition to the States from "impairing the obligations of contracts" as cited in Article 1 Section 10. The assault on this prohibition is nearing a full success, thanks to the acquiescence of the courts.

Chapter 33
Line of Succession

Given the limited scope of the federal government as envisioned in the Constitution, continuity of government was only essential to insure the functions necessary such as the defense of the country did not lapse during the time its functionaries were transitioning from the replacement of old members to new because it was never assumed that people who were voted in would be automatically reelected. Except for the President and Vice President. other elected members of the government were not needed full time to administer the government's ongoing affairs. In short, the position of politician was part time and could be practiced only if one was prepared to cede the time from their main occupation. This limited the field to retirees, self-employed individuals whose clients were one time such as lawyers or members of a family business or partnership who could remand their contribution to their progeny or partners while they tended to the business of government.

The changing of the guard still required time for individuals to settle their affairs before making the trip to Philadelphia and later Washington D. C. which in those days took several days in itself for travel and the framers were looking to the time when more distant States would enter the Union.

Improvements in transportation and communication and the fact national politician by 1933 was a full-time job requiring almost no transition time except for those elected for the first time the "lame duck" period could have been reduced to zero without disrupting the continuity of functioning of the federal government. In fact, the government bureaucracy can and has functioned without political leadership but this would admit that political leadership is actually unnecessary but would not be acceptable if it were being administered by members of the opposition according to their agenda. A problem neatly avoided under a monarchy or a dictatorship.

Neither political party could sidestep the advantages afforded the other during a lame duck session if they were perchance enabled to replace their power structure so a compromise was need. It is similar to the argument over term limits wherein the only benefit gained is that it forces those who need or want to steal less time to do it. And so we have an amendment that produces the same result with only lesser time for a party who holds both the Congress and the Presidency to do their mischief.

In simple terms, it was an unnecessary amendment but one that was a reminder of the politicization of the federal government, as if such was necessary.

Chapter 34
Repeal of Prohibition

The twenty-first amendment to the U. S. Constitution repealed the unconstitutional amendment XVIII. After nearly 13 years the Congress finally realized that when you do things that are not permitted under the Constitution or are actually prohibited, bad things happen. The lesson what short lived because a similar tactic was tried with tobacco, another potentially addictive substance. This time however the miscreants were allowed to continue producing the product but severely punished in the pocketbook for doing so. Or, so the politicians made you think.

Granted, most of the tobacco companies know, like those who produce alcohol, that more than moderate use would result in addiction and worse, health consequences. Denying such facts runs in the face of irrefutable evidence from smoker autopsies linking smoking to lung cancer.

An aside here will illustrate the lengths lawyers and particularly lawyer politicians will rig the rules in their favor. In criminal cases the accused has a right to engage an attorney to assist in his defense. There is nothing in the Constitution that claims a person to be innocent until proven guilty. It has however been a fundamental right since ancient time to protect the innocent from the State. Unless caught in the act or confessing to its perpetration it is harder to prove guilt than it is innocence so the procedure when the first two alternatives are prima facie admission of guilt is to submit evidence to a Grand Jury of a person's guilt in order to subject someone to a trial by a jury or a judge. The accused then has the option to submit his evidence of innocence to a judge or a jury. When the Congress drafted Article VI as an amendment to the Constitution they reiterated the right of an accused to have a speedy and public trial by an impartial jury of his peers and among other things the assistance of counsel for his defense. Each of these rights may be waived by the accused and nowhere is it stipulated that the State is required to pay for anything accept the accused rights to obtain witnesses on his behalf.

Not so in the case of civil offenses or torts where the disagreement is among individuals and no criminal offense has been committed but is strictly a monetary claim of damages either for failure to perform or to not perform as stipulated in a contract. In this case the accused is given no right to a speedy trial and is presumed guilty unless they can prove otherwise. When you do not have a right it is difficult to waive it and if you are assumed guilty the size of the judgement will increase on the basis of how much emotion can be dredged up in support of claimant. This reversal of justice has proven a gold mine for tort lawyers reinforcing the meaning of the phrase, "he who has the gold makes the rules".

The foregoing provided the government with a ready means to appear to appease the public by financially punishing the tobacco companies. The truth is it is now almost impossible for anyone who continues to smoke to collect damages from the tobacco companies and the so-called settlements they paid went mostly into the pockets of lawyers and subsequent purchasers of tobacco products ultimately paid the amount of these settlements in the increased price of the product. Asbestos manufacturers were not so fortunate even though the acquisition of asbestoses was not deliberate on the part of these manufacturers. The consequences of these settlements bankrupted all of the asbestos manufacturers, fattened the wallets of the tort lawyers but did not cure those afflicted.

Narcotics is now the culprit in a similar case of the abuse of habit forming or addictive drugs. They are already banned that is a position the federal government nor States were given in their constitutions by the people. If the State has the power to ban anything is has the power to ban everything as it suits those making the laws. Murder and theft are banned but they are still perpetrated.

Chapter 35
Term Limits

The 22nd amendment to the U. S. Constitution prevents anyone from serving more than two terms in the office. The movement to limit the term of President is not new and was considered as early in the framing of the Constitution. The four-year term was a compromise as there were some who wanted the President to serve for life, in essence turning it into a monarchy. Since Washington's time most Presidents respected the two-term limit, primarily because the office was usually held by men who were already into their senior years and past their prime to withstand the rigors of the office.

Franklin Roosevelt broke the precedent, and was actually in his fourth term when he met his untimely death. That experience and the fact that he had poorly prepared his Vice President to assume the office and in the middle of a war further demonstrated the feasibility of limiting the term of the President's office.

Unlike a private corporation, it is the people who select those who govern them. The reason is they are the customers of the government's services. Customers of private corporations can only display their dissatisfaction or satisfaction with the products or services being provided by buying or not buying them. In the public sector, you have to live what you get regardless of whether you voted for the person or not and in a democracy 51% can, under our economic system, deny much of the nation's wealth to the other 49%. Their only recourse is to emigrate to where their lot is better, if they can, or revolt and turn the tables on their former persecutors.

It matters little who occupies the office because the entrenched bureaucracy can and does run the government, just as subordinate personnel in a private company run it in absence of active intervention by its CEO and only when it results in potential failure is the culture of the organization changed. It was Alfred Sloan, the CEO of General Motors who claimed a new leader had 5 years to institute changes and see them to fruition. My question to Mr. Sloan is if the organization is successful there should be no need for change. As a matter of fact, Sloan's leadership resulted in GM's divisions competing with each other and led to near bankruptcy. General Electric, on the other hand, has maintained the same successful strategy for years and their grooming of people to implement that strategy has resulted in those who were passed over for the top job, becoming CEOs of other companies.

The U. S. Government, in taking on the posture of a benefactor of last resorts, implements policies of cradle to grave benefits for those who cannot afford them or don't want to pay for them. It has created an entitlement society that neither party dares to unravel. No new party would have a chance to challenge this if their platform even hints at abandonment of these entitlements. The entrenched bureaucracy is perfectly capable of implementing this and is eager to do so because their jobs depend on not changing.

It is these entitlements and the economic system employed that makes them necessary and little can or will be done to prevent the ultimate demise of the present government and if another government adopts the same economic system, all that will happen will be but a repeat of the same.

Chapter 37
District of Columbia

Amendment XXIII to the U. S. Constitution gives voting rights in federal elections to residents of the District of Columbia. The district was envisioned in the original document as a place to be carved out of one of the States who would concede it to the federal authority. As we know the seating of it was itself a compromise wherein James Madison, Alexander Hamilton and Thomas Jefferson agreed that in exchange of their sharing of the war debts, Virginia and Maryland would cede land to the federal authority. It would in essence make the people currently living on the ceded lands stateless but still citizens of the United States. This dilemma could have easily been solved because the borders of what became the district were well known and those citizens could have retained all of the rights of the States who had previously owned the land.

The underlying factor that results in differences has to do with the economic system that has been adopted by every government in recorded history. That is that individuals or groups of individual's own nature's assets. When man was nomadic and roamed the earth in search of food, ownership of anything was determined by what man did with nature's assets that were free to all and the only thing that could be stolen was what man made from those assets. When man found he could tame nature and no longer had to roam the earth, its production in the form of food belonged to a society as a whole who could defend it from those who might covet it. If man realized that nature's assets, even those enhanced, could sustain only so many people he might have reduced the population increase by restraining himself to replacement only. The consequences of this failure has manifested itself ever since the inability of societies to constrain their membership to the assets available in the land they occupy.

Having denied those who would reside on government land the right of representation the State governments have carried it to its extreme denying the right to vote in State elections to residents of all federal lands and in some cases students who are in the State only temporarily. The federal government has denied it to citizens of its territories, in particular Puerto Rico, American Samoa and at one time the Panama Canal Zone and the Philippines prior to their return to the indigenous population. They have not exempted them from taxes.

Government is simply a substitution of the rights of parents to discipline their children. The children do not get to vote on who their parents are. As Madison, has stipulated, there would be no need for government if everyone was an angel and there was no stealing. The only need for government is the apprehension and punishment of thieves because the owners are incapable of apprehending one who flees without totally disrupting their lives. If caught in the act or attempting theft the one from whom something is being stolen has a right to defend his property up to an including killing the thief.

The law in biblical times was the Ten Commandments that is ostensibly about stealing, the punishment for which was death by stoning. If you read Deuteronomy, the Old Testament book that cites the Ten Commandments you will also find that a family who could not get their son to obey the rules of the parents, could take him before the elders, declare they could not control the actions of their son and he would thereupon be stoned to death.

The purpose of this lengthy digression is to demonstrate that rather than a digression it is the establishment of the only reason government exists at all and has taken its present form is because the human race has evolved into one where nature's assets are no longer the property of everyone but a select few and as the saying goes, he who has the gold (property) makes the rules and those rules, in the United States derived from the home country England that gave bankers the permission to legally steal through usury and then in the Roosevelt era this permission was granted to organized labor and indirectly to corporate management when corporate ownership was diversified to anyone with a partial interest in its ownership and their only concern was the dividend stream they needed others to control.

The preservation of this system is almost guaranteed because those who benefit far outnumber those who do not. Government breaks down in this scenario, not when those at the bottom end of the distribution do not get enough exchange to survive but when it has to start cutting back on the shares that are being distributed. I cite Greece and the state employees of Wisconsin as examples.

For additional details on why and how this economic system evolved and will eventually result in a premature demise of the human race I refer you to my book "The Real Economy". It comes complete with a method that will not prevent the demise of the human race but remove the inequality of the present system and thereby extend the duration of period of life of humans on the planet.

Chapter 38
Presidential Succession

The reason for this provision is not that the framers of the document hadn't given it any thought. Remember they had just gotten through a war that nearly was lost. It certainly was not continuity of law making, because bills could become law without the President's approval. All that was required was they be unattended to for 10 days after submittal. This is why no President whose Congress is of another party stays unavailable for more than 10 days, in order to thwart a renegade Congress' from passing bills in his absence. No bill could be considered that urgent that it could not be withheld from submittal until the President regained his capacity. Being good parliamentarians, the framers could have written in that the President could delegate his authority to the Vice President but such a situation has so many pitfalls that it is merely an understanding that if the President cannot act, in his absence, the Vice President assumes his authority.

The key provision in the amendment is Section 4 that allows the Vice President and a majority of the President's principle officers or such other body as Congress may provide declares the President unable to discharge his duties. The Vice President shall immediately assume the powers and duties as Acting President. In other words, Commander and Chief of the Army and Navy and the militia when called into service by the Congress and the enforcement of all federal law. None of the latter are again urgent, even in war time and the established bureaucracy both military and civilian are capable of carrying on without the personal attention of the President.

It should be remembered that at the time this amendment became law the only real power the President had was not in making law but enforcing those he liked and not enforcing those he did not like. His control of the military remained intact and was greater than ever because there was now a permanent cadre of volunteer troops, sailors and airmen who were armed with sophisticated weapons and a far superior force than was available to George Washington. His only problem was he could not employ them except on Congressional authorization, except as in the prohibition to the States; "unless actually invaded, or in such imminent danger as will not admit of delay". Pretty loose constraints and rightly so and even these constraints are not applicable to the President. The Congress has attempted to restrict this authority with War Powers Acts but none of them prohibit completely any action by the President should he choose to exceed the restrictions. Again, the end justifies the means and if success ensues the overstepping is ignored..

The deeper purpose, I believe, was to enable a so called "palace coup" in the event a rogue President should happen to get elected or stray thereafter from the party line. It was heretofore entirely unnecessary to enlist the aid of cabinet officers because the President rarely got to pick individuals of his own choosing and simply accepted those put forward by the party. It is very similar to the way Vice Presidents have been chosen.

This party safety valve may not be available to the Republicans in the case of Donald Trump. He picked his own Vice President and he appears on the way to picking cabinet officers in the same way, loyal to Trump and his agenda and not necessarily that of the old Republican Guard that has now been emasculated by the members of the Tea Party and avid Trump supporters.

Chapter 39
Universal Suffrage

The twenty-sixth amendment to the U. S. Constitution provides for the vote of 18-year old's, what may be the last vestige of voter discrimination remaining until a sufficient number of resident non-citizens assemble as a mob and clamor for equal "rights". Surprisingly there are many legitimate citizens who believe they should.

The metamorphosis of what was originally a privilege into a right is personified by that leading to universal suffrage. That is, the right of everyone over a certain age (maturity) to vote. One need remember that the American colonists had no representation in the English Parliament but they were subject to English taxes, the reason and the amount of those taxes in which they had no say. They did have local governments, subordinate of course to that of the government in England and in that government, not all colonists were represented. Those represented were one of their own and they were defined by wealth, either in land or income and these were defined so as to keep out indentured servants, slaves and men who worked for wages or salaries that did not achieve a certain level. During that time there were not too many and few paid taxes they had no cause to complain.

As is the case in the economic system all governments have adopted, time and the addition of those who did not meet the initial qualifications continued to rise and a fixed dollar value of worth in order to vote would have had to increase to keep pace with inflation and as a consequence would deny suffrage to more and more of an ever-growing population. A real example would be if the worth limit were set at $5,000, I would have just qualified to vote when I was offered my first job as a college graduate. To deny the vote to anyone who is not a college graduate today that limit would have to be set at about $30,000 simply due to the inflation of the dollar. This criterion would in effect deny suffrage to over half the working population. This presents a dilemma to the politicians in that they must appear to represent more of the people or face the possibility of revolt over taxation.

The solution to this dilemma was to make it appear that the masses were being represented by placating them on one hand from the treasury while screwing them with the other so as to continue to provide for the minority rich that give them the wherewithal to continue the process. This process has been made necessary by the economic system chosen to measure the economy and its activity. So long as we remain tied to gold, even though its supply is dwindling, populations are increasing and there will become a time when the quantity being distributed by government will not be sufficient to purchase what is actually a dwindling food supply.

It is too long an analysis of how we got to this point and where we are ultimately headed but I explain it in greater detail in my book "The Real Economy". It contains a system that will correct the faults in the current system, that has caused all previous societies to collapse or disperse.

www.ingramcontent.com/pod-product-compliance
Lightning Source LLC
Chambersburg PA
CBHW051216170526
45166CB00005B/1930